————— PEOPLE AND COMMUNICATION —————

Series Editors:
PETER CLARKE   *University of Southern California*
F. GERALD KLINE   *University of Minnesota*

Volumes in this series:

JEROME JOHNSTON
JAMES S. ETTEMA

POSITIVE IMAGES

BREAKING STEREOTYPES WITH CHILDREN'S TELEVISION

Foreword by ALETHA C. HUSTON

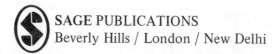

SAGE PUBLICATIONS
Beverly Hills / London / New Delhi

Copyright © 1982 by Sage Publications, Inc.

For information address:

SAGE Publications, Inc.
275 South Beverly Drive
Beverly Hills, California 90212

SAGE Publications India Pvt. Ltd.
C-236 Defence Colony
New Delhi 110 024, India

SAGE Publications Ltd
28 Banner Street
London EC1Y 8QE, England

Printed in the United States of America

Library of Congress Cataloging in Publication Data

Johnston, Jerome.
Ettema, James S.
   Positive Images: Breaking Stereotypes with
     Children's Television.
   (People and communication : v. 14)
   Bibliography: p.
   1. Freestyle (Television program) 2. Television programs for children — United
States. 3. Television in education — United States. 4. Sex role. 5. Ethnic attitudes.
6. Stereotype (Psychology). I. Ettema, James S.   II. Title.   III. Series.
PN1992.77.F733J6   791.45'72   82-3356
ISBN 0-8039-0384-7   AACR2
ISBN 0-8039-0385-5 (pbk.)

FIRST PRINTING 83-4052

Contents

To our parents
Joseph and Janice Johnston
John and Marilyn Ettema

Foreword

The period from 1965 to 1980 witnessed the growth and decline of efforts to create television programs which were designed to promote cognitive and social development of children. Visionaries had talked of the great potential in the television medium for education of children, but very few attempts to realize that potential had been made in its first thirty years of existence. Several historical trends in the 1960s coincided to make possible serious efforts to produce good television for children. The national conscience and awareness of social inequities had been raised by the civil rights movement and by the general tone of concern for human welfare that pervaded our political and social rhetoric. Head Start and other "compensatory education" programs were one means of ameliorating the inequality. Partly because government and private funds were available, educators turned also to television as a tool for enhancing early cognitive development. One of the earliest products of their efforts, *Sesame Street,* succeeded in drawing audiences and teaching intellectual skills beyond anyone's most optimistic predictions. It broke a major barrier to commercial educational television by showing that the purposive programming could be entertaining and fun, and, most important, that it could compete for a significant portion of the viewing audience.

While cognitive and intellectual skills were understandably the major focus of many planned programs, social-emotional development was also espoused as a goal for television. Researchers in the field turned from studying antisocial content to prosocial behavior, showing that children would imitate cooperation and helping just as they imitated aggression. Commercial programmers eagerly, but cautiously, embraced the idea of making prosocial programs as a way of avoiding harmful behavioral effects. At the same time, they responded to political pressure from minority groups with some attempts to portray blacks in more favorable and less stereotyped roles than had previously been the case.

The television series *Freestyle* was conceived in this atmosphere of optimism and social change. The women's movement followed the civil rights movement, and educators became aware of inequities for women as well. In the case of women, however, the problem lay not in differential opportunity for gaining early intellectual skills, but in early socialization of attitudes, interests, behavioral skills, and long-term goals. Women were socialized to expect a subservient, dependent role, either as an unpaid housewife or as a low-level worker in the labor market. Men were socialized to expect to be leaders, to seek high levels of achievement, and to be superior to their women. In fact, although women have been entering the labor market in increasing numbers for most of the twentieth century, their average income has remained steadily at about 60 percent of men's average income. The average female college graduate earns a salary equivalent to the average male with an eighth-grade education. Of course, minority group women have even lower incomes than white women; they suffer the disadvantages imposed by both gender and race.

The idea for *Freestyle* was developed by staff in the National Institute for Education (NIE). Agencies such as NIE properly viewed their role as assessing national needs and priorities and attempting to stimulate research and development in areas they deemed most important. Staff members of the Career Education section of NIE issued a Request for Proposal (RFP) for a television series that would be designed to reduce the influence of sex and ethnic group stereotyping on children's career interests. The grant was awarded to a consortium consisting of professional television producers, curriculum design specialists, community-based activists, and academic researchers. At least six major private and public institutions were represented.

In this book, Jerome Johnston and James Ettema trace the evolution and development of *Freestyle* through its long period of planning and formative research to the summative evaluation which was carried out under Johnston's direction. The first part of the book is an interesting case study of the development process, with all its growing pains, of new educational experiment created from scratch. The funding agency had the foresight to include a "chronicler" of the process. Ettema spent many months attending the meetings of the various planning groups, reading drafts of materials, and taking careful notes on events as they occurred. The data presented here are primarily from his observations, not from second-hand reports of parties who might have widely varying perceptions.

What we learn from the historical record is how much time, effort, and energy are required to create a team that can work together effectively and efficiently in spite of the fact that its members spring from different backgrounds with different professional languages and orientations. There is always a tension in educational television between the creative, artistic goals of the writers and producers on the one hand, and the educational objectives generated by developmental psychologists and educators on the other. The artists want to make their product aesthetically pleasing, entertaining, and dramatically interesting; the educators want to communicate a concept clearly, avoid complications or ambiguities, and match the child's level of understanding. In my opinion, one of the major reasons that *Freestyle* finally satisfied the goals of both groups was the fact that the executive producer could talk and think in both languages. His earlier experience with *Sesame Street* provided a model for integrating educational objectives with artistic goals, and he quickly learned and understood the major ideas about sex stereotyping and pre-occupational interests that were the core curriculum of *Freestyle*.

Still a third set of forces influencing the development process was the social-political concerns of a variety of community groups. Although the initial proposal emphasized both ethnic and gender stereotypes, it was clear to everyone that a single television series could not deal effectively with both. Many people involved in the formation of specific goals for the program were veterans of battles about priorities in other educational efforts, and they did not want to see this one hampered by divisive conflict. The resolution, which satisfied most people, was to make sex stereotypes the major focus, and to make ethnic group differences in sex stereotypes a secondary emphasis. One rationale was the fact that many educational television programs had been designed to correct ethnic stereotypes, but none had previously (or since) been explicitly focused on gender stereotypes.

Formative research has become an expected part of educational technology, particularly educational television. The formative research for *Freestyle,* carried out by members of the Annenberg School of Communication at the University of Southern California, consisted of extensive and comprehensive reviews of the literature on sex typing as well as studies designed to test specific techniques to be used in the television programs. The literature search and conceptual summary was required because, as Johnston and Ettema point out, the consortium lacked experts on the topic of sex typing and sex roles. Consultants with such expertise were imported early in the process, primarily at the instigation of the Project Officer from NIE. Nevertheless, someone on the primary consortium team had to know the developmental literature, and the task fell to the formative research team. In this volume, the formative research process is described only briefly, partly because it is presented in detail in another book (Williams et al., 1981).

Summative evaluations of the *Freestyle* series was a major component of the original plan. Following the model established for *Sesame Street* and *Electric Company,* the summative evaluation was carried out by a staff and an institution which were independent from those involved in production. Its major components, as described in the second half of this book, were evaluation of audience appeal and assessment of how well the series achieved its educational objectives. In order to carry out this assignment while maintaining the required "neutrality," Jerome Johnston and the research staff at the Institute for Social Research at the University of Michigan had to tread a narrow path that permitted sufficient involvement with the production process to plan a relevant and sensible evaluation without compromising their objectivity as "outsiders" in the consortium team.

Several significant themes emerge from the summative evaluation which bear on other efforts to use television for affective or prosocial education. Children enjoyed the programs and watched them frequently at home as well as in the classroom. One immediately wonders why this kind of programming is not more prominent in the offerings of commercial or even public television. Perhaps one answer is that a series has to build a following gradually. Thirteen episodes are hardly enough to acquaint members of the viewing audience with the format and characters. Yet, television production is so expensive that it proved impossible to find money for more programs in the series.

Johnston and Ettema summarize the successes and failures of the series in meeting educational objectives very concisely. When used in the classroom with supplementary discussion and print materials, the programs led to changes in children's stereotypes and beliefs about the sex-appropriateness of activities and interests such as mechanics, nurturing activities, and athletics. Children's own interests were less clearly influenced, but girls who saw the program did express increased interest in mechanical and athletic activities. Knowledge and attitudes about more subtle behavioral skills, such as leadership, independence, and moderate risk-taking were not readily influenced by the series. Such skills are less concrete and more difficult to conceptualize than activities such as art or child care. It may be, however, that the effects of portraying such behaviors on television occur more at the level of subtle behavioral changes than at the level of conceptual understanding or verbalized attitudes measured in the evaluation. In other studies of prosocial television, conceptual understanding and behavioral adoption are often relatively independent. Or it may be that such behavioral skills were not affected by the televised presentations.

When the thirteen shows were merely viewed and not discussed, the effects were much more limited. Yet a few effects were quite large, and all were in the desired direction. These confirm the potential of good television drama to bring about positive change in children.

The authors have integrated their mass of data in a coherent, organized fashion that makes it easy to read and to extract the major points. They also balance the careful presentation of data with thoughtful speculation about the importance and significance of the findings. Their ideas about the future of planned programming for children make valuable reading for anyone interested in that area. We have reached an era in the early 1980s where the public mood is very different from the 1960s. Funding for planned programming has always come primarily from government sources — both federal and state. Major reductions in that funding and in overall support for public television mean that we will see few if any new productions of purposive programming for education and development of children unless commercial producers can be induced to put some resources into that area. Nevertheless, the lessons about the successes and failures may provide guidance for future efforts, whenever they occur. One of those lessons is that sporadic funding for specific productions is much less efficient and economical than continuing funding which can maintain an organization to carry on long-term efforts for programming. Part of the reason *Freestyle* went through such a long and rocky development effort was that a complex organization had to be built from scratch. There was a model from Children's Television Workshop, but the executive producer was the only person with experience in that model. A large and diverse group of people and institutions had to develop a working organization at the same time they were trying to develop a television show. "Start up" time is always large in a new enterprise; a second series or more *Freestyle* shows could have been designed in half the time by the same group. The same comments apply to building a viewing audience and to building familiarity with the program among station executives and other gatekeepers. The initial stages are slow and painful; the benefits accumulate. Continuing organizations for the production of planned programming could use funds more efficiently for producing good programs that have continuity over time. Johnston and Ettema have provided us with an excellent analysis of a creative effort. Perhaps sometime in the future, we will use their ideas when we give priority to children's intellectual and social-emotional needs once more.

Aletha C. Huston
University of Kansas

Preface

This book is about the award-winning television series *Free-style*—an ambitious effort to create television to alter children's stereotypes about sex roles. It is largely a success story and as such it serves as a model for others who would produce television to teach positive social values.

Over the last decade large amounts of money — largely federal dollars — have been invested in purposive programming for children. This includes such series as *3-2-1 Contact, Villa Alegre, Zoom,* and *Feeling Free.* Like these other series, *Freestyle* was seen as a much-needed intervention for a particular problem. Unique to *Freestyle* was the conception of the funder, the National Institute of Education (NIE), that the project was an experiment that could inform others about the potential of television to achieve social goals. NIE allocated an unusually large amount for two studies — one a study of the creative process that led to the series; the other a study of the effects of the series on its audience. Those findings were made available in 1980 in two technical reports (Johnston et al., 1980; Ettema, 1980). The present book is an attempt to simplify the findings of that research and present it in a form that is readable to a broad audience. Further, to increase its usefulness for future endeavors we have tried to show how events and decisions in the production process relate to changes in the viewing audience. We think such a book is needed because *Freestyle's* successes — and failures — can be very instructive to those who would fund or produce prosocial television in the future.

We are convinced of its potential, but more needs to be learned to make it an even more effective tool.

Throughout this book we refer to the *Freestyle* enterprise as an experiment in "prosocial" television. Some might argue that changing sex-role stereotypes does not constitute a "prosocial" intervention. But so much of the attention in television research is focused on television's potential for antisocial effects that we find the term "prosocial" convenient to refer to television designed to promote a particular set of social values.

To study *Freestyle's* effects on children, we mounted an unusually large research effort involving seven cities, 88 schools, and more than 6000 children. Large amounts of data were collected from students and teachers. To produce this book we explored these data in depth, but hardly exhausted them. There is ample room for other researchers to discover important relationships. To assist in this, the data have been archived by the Inter-University Consortium for Political and Social Research (ICPSR) at the University of Michigan. Information on data tapes and documentation can be obtained by writing: Director, Member Services, ICPSR, P.O. Box 1248, Ann Arbor, MI 48106.

This account of *Freestyle* is ours. But it is based on the actions and products of others, many of whom deserve mention. A series of events and actors in the early 1970s led to the blueprint and funding of *Freestyle*. Under contract with NIE, Aimee Dorr and Gerry Lesser wrote a review that was very influential in the selection of television as the medium for altering sex-role stereotypes. Mary Lou Randour and Bob Wise at NIE conceived of the particulars of the television series with its many component parts. Bob Wise in particular insisted on the inclusion of a large evaluation component. A host of people were involved in the design and production of *Freestyle*. Of particular note among these are Norton Wright at KCET-TV (Los Angeles), Fred Williams and Bob LaRose at the University of Southern California, and Judy Anderson at

Science Research Associates. At Los Angeles County Schools were Pat Seeley, Pat Whitman, Jo Bonita Perez, and Bob Gerletti. Aletha Huston at the University of Kansas suggested the themes for a number of the programs.

At the University of Michigan, Terry Davidson, Chris Lux, Greg Herr, and Linda Shepard worked for several years executing the original evaluation study. Jean Holther edited, typed, and coordinated this book though several years of manuscript development.

The research design and data analysis profited from the wisdom of many researchers who made important contributions to our thinking during the last six years. These include Jerry Bachman, Sam Ball, Terry Davidson, Aimee Dorr, Keith Mielke, Joe Pleck, and Saul Rockman.

Finally, we owe a special debt to our families who have been indelibly marked by the lost evenings and weekends and countless periods of inattention as our minds were absorbed with making sense out of the whole *Freestyle* experience.

Jerome Johnston
University of Michigan

James S. Ettema
University of Minnesota

Chapter 1

INTRODUCTION TO *FREESTYLE*
A Strategy for Prosocial Television

Christine at thirteen is keenly interested in auto mechanics and in finding a summer job. There's a chance to combine these interests — a job at Mat's service station — but first Chris must face crusty old Mat.

"I'd like that summer job you've got there," Chris says pointing to the sign which says "Boy Wanted."

Mat looks at the sign and then at Chris. "What does that sign say? Go ahead and read it to me."

Chris hesitates. "It says there is a position open."

"No, that isn't what it says," Mat snaps. "Try again. And don't try to be smart-alecky with old Mat Morgan."

Mr. Morgan, I didn't come here to be teased," Chris responds. "I am good with cars and I have come to take that job."

Chris assertively stakes a claim to the job, but Mat is unyielding. "The very idea, a girl working in a gas station. It's ridiculous," snorts Mat as he walks away leaving Chris at the gas pumps.

Suddenly, a whole caravan of cars and campers descends on the station. Mat returns to pump gas, but is swamped by the rush. The drivers become impatient. Chris watches for a moment and then decides to take a risk. While Mat is inside making change, Chris unhooks the hose from the car that was just filled and motions it forward so the next car can move up. She takes the order and begins to fill the tank. Mat returns, but before he can shoo her away the first customer demands his change. Chris continues to service the cars and Mat continues to make change. The pressure from the customers keeps them both locked into their tasks. Finally, Chris and Mat are left standing in the suddenly quiet service station.

"That sign has been in the window for two weeks," Chris says.

Mat scowls, "Okay, okay, okay, okay. You did it. So?"

"So I've got the job. Right?"

"Wrong." But then Mat pauses. "Okay, okay, okay, okay. But if you stick it out to the end of the week I'll eat my hat."

Chris does stick it out. She works hard, increases her mechanical expertise by assisting Dave, the mechanic, and after a time she even gains Mat's grudging respect. And one day when Mat and Dave have to leave the station, she is left in charge.

Soon Chris has her first customer, a salesman with motor trouble. Chris' quick diagnosis of the problem and her assurance that she can do the job quickly convince the salesman to let her do it. Chris goes to work coolly and professionally, but this time she has taken too big a risk. When Mat and Dave return Chris is standing amid a pile of bolts and brackets holding a radiator in her arms.

"What are you doing with *that*?" Mat growls.

"Well, Mr. Lang here needs a new flywheel and the only way I could get to it was by removing the radiator and . . ."

Dave interrupts, "Chris, that's not how you do it. The engine's got to be pulled out for a job like that. This is a real mess now."

"No one else was here!" Chris responds.

"That's no excuse, Chris. If you don't know how to do something, ask for help. You should have called me on the phone. You had the number."

"I know I can put it back together," Chris says weakly.

"Who's going to pay for the orders I'm losing because of her?" the salesman grumbles to Mat.

"I must've been out of my mind to hire you," Mat growls at Chris.

Chris clutches the radiator grimly and says nothing.

A class of fourth graders has been intently watching Chris' predicament on the television set in their classroom. When "To Be Continued" appears over the image of a forlorn Chris the class is very silent for an instant. Then it explodes.

"I told you so," says one of the boys.

"She CAN get it back together," retorts a girl.

Everyone is talking at once, but soon the teacher intervenes to begin a discussion of the lesson to be learned from Chris' adventure — the difference between reasonable and unreasonable risks.

Watching the children watch television is the executive producer of the show. The show is one of three experimental pilots for an educational series called *Freestyle*. This pilot has been created to explore the use of drama to achieve the series goal — countering sex-role stereotypes and expanding career awareness among 9- to 12-year-olds. The other pilots have explored the use of music, comedy, and animation. The executive producer is here to see for himself how children — particularly boys — respond to this approach.

As the class discussion turns to the idea of female auto mechanics one of the fourth graders whispers to the executive producer, "Did you make this show?"

"Yes."

"I'll give you a quarter if you tell me what happens."

A good deal of work by the formative researchers is still to be done before one of the three pilots is selected as the prototype for the series, but right now the executive producer has very little doubt which it will be.

THE *FREESTYLE* MESSAGES AND MATERIALS

Dramas like Chris's summer job did indeed become the basis of the *Freestyle* experience for children. After three years of planning, research, and production the completed series includes thirteen half-hour dramas featuring youngsters and adults engaged in activities, behaviors, and roles that, until only recently, would have been considered nontraditional for their sex. These nontraditional pursuits are clustered into the series' three content themes:

(1) *Childhood Pre-Occupational Activities.* These are activities in which 9- to 12-year-olds engage and that may lead to specific career interests. Featured activities include mechanics, science, and athletics for girls, and nurturant activities for boys.

(2) *Childhood Behavioral Skills.* These are skills 9- to 12-year-olds can begin to develop and that are useful in later careers. Featured behavioral skills include leadership, independence, assertiveness, and reasonable risk-taking for girls, helping skills for boys, and cooperation for both sexes.

(3) *Adult Work And Family Roles.* These include frequently stereotyped adult activities, both in the home (e.g., child care, cooking) and in the work place (e.g., specific jobs).

The activities, behaviors, and roles are modeled by attractive and competent characters of all races. All of the characters, like Chris, have trials and tribulations because of their nontraditional choices, but in the end, they are rewarded. Chris's story, for example, comes to a happy end when she refuses to be defeated by her mistake, returns to work, improves further her mechanical expertise, and saves the day in a classic television fashion the next time there is trouble. In another episode, Marcus and Walter volunteer at a senior citizens' center. Marcus puts his organizational skills to work and figures he will have the seniors' recreational program in shape in no time. He's surprised to find, however, that the seniors respond to his arbitrary and overtaxing schedule by walking out on his project, a craft sale. Marcus and Walter then learn from the center's occupational therapist and the seniors themselves the importance of fully understanding the needs of others when trying to help them. The seniors return and the sale succeeds brilliantly.

Through these dramas, *Freestyle* offers a glimpse into an idealized world — a world in which the old stereotypes about boys' and girls' abilities and skills are no longer true. The world of *Freestyle* has been created to be somewhat at odds with children's own "real world" and with many other television worlds, but it has also been created to be internally consistent and true to its own non-stereotyped principles. The *Freestyle* strategy for countering sex-role stereotypes and expanding career awareness is, in essence, to do what television does best

— construct a coherent and compelling alternative reality with the potential to become the audience's own.

Thus, *Freestyle* refuses to simply rail against the evils of stereotypes and chooses instead to model positive alternatives. But even more than providing positive role models, it sets out to provide specific information on how to become like the models. The episode of Chris's summer job not only portrays the value of reasonable risks and the dangers of unreasonable ones, but also offers children some help in distinguishing between the two. Similarly, the episode of Marcus and Walter's volunteer project shows that nurturance is more than simply being nice by discussing the importance of learning the needs and abilities of others when trying to help them. *Freestyle* sets out to take the mystery out of nontraditional pursuits, and to show children that anyone can do them if they really want to and try hard enough.

Freestyle uses several specific strategies to harness television's power. One of the strategies is the dramatic structure of each episode. Most of the episodes focus on a behavioral skill central to the plot of the story. The story of Chris's summer job, for example, turns on her risk-taking, both reasonable and unreasonable. Marcus and Walter's experience at the senior citizen's center turns on their acquisition of helping skills. In the jargon of the *Freestyle* developers, these behavioral skills constitute the "figure" of an episode that is set against the "ground" of some pre-occupational activity or adult role. Chris's risk-taking is, for example, set against the ground of mechanics while Marcus and Walter's development of helping skills is set against the ground of a specific nurturing activity, volunteer work with senior citizens.

To make the point of each episode more explicit and accessible to the 9- to 12-year-old audience, scenes in which characters label and discuss the skills and activities have been written into the story. These are called "Ah-ha!" scenes because the developers hope that upon seeing them children will exclaim, "Ah-ha! Now I understand."

Another structural feature of the dramas is noteworthy. Each drama runs one half-hour, but is divisible into two quarter-hour chapters. The half-hour episodes, intended for prime-time and after-school broadcast, are standard program length for these time periods. The quarter-hour chapters, intended for instructional use, are amenable to teachers' schedules. When aired as two separate quarter-hour chapters, the first chapter ends with a cliffhanger and the second chapter resolves the dilemma; when aired as a single half-hour episode, the two chapters flow together without interruption. Chris's auto repair disaster is a vivid example of a cliffhanger.

Freestyle, like other series intended for instructional use, is accompanied by a teacher's guide. The guide includes pre-viewing warm-up activities for each chapter, post-viewing discussion topics and exercises, and follow-up activities and projects. The follow-up ideas include suggestions for "infusing" the lessons, television shows, and printed materials into other curriculum areas if and when teachers cannot devote time to career awareness or countering stereotypes as a separate activity. The guide suggests, for example, that a language arts assignment be an essay on one of the shows, while a math assignment be the preparation of graphs showing the percentage of men and women in various occupations. In this way the lessons and materials of *Freestyle* can become a part of the ongoing instruction in basic skills. The teacher's guide, along with the complementary student activity booklet are, then, designed both to help teachers clarify and expand the lessons and to help them fit the materials into their curriculum needs and constraints.

In summary, *Freestyle* is an interesting and important experiment in educational television because it attempts to present sophisticated, yet accessible, prosocial messages in the form of television drama. The strategy is to embed the messages within compelling stories — to make the message and story one in the same — and yet to make the messages readily comprehensible through such devices as the figure/ground dramatic structure, the "Ah-ha!" scenes, and classroom discussion. *Freestyle* thus explores new approaches to a basic problem of educational television — the synthesis of education and entertainment.

THE *FREESTYLE* FUNDAMENTALS

The *Freestyle* strategy, messages, and materials grew from four fundamental ideas. The first was the goal of countering children's sex-role stereotypes and the second was the concept of using an entertaining and educational television series to achieve that goal. The third was an outline of a process for making such a television series, and the fourth was a commitment to evaluating the effectiveness of the whole enterprise.

The goal, the first of the fundamental *Freestyle* ideas, was formulated by staff of the National Institute of Education (NIE), the funder of the series. According to NIE's original statement, the goal was to "expand the career awareness of 4th to 6th graders by making sex and ethnicity less significant predictors of pre-occupational (or occupational) knowledge, interest and preferences" (National Institute of Education, 1975).

In this statement were several key ideas. One was the concept of career awareness that, according to NIE, includes both interest in particular occupations and knowledge about those occupations, such as their demands and rewards. For elementary-age children, career awareness includes "pre-occupational" as well as occupational interests and knowledge. A pre-occupational interest, for example, is a fascination with mechanical devices, while pre-occupational knowledge includes awareness of mechanical careers. Such pre-occupational interests and knowledge are formed long before the selection of a particular job and serve as a guide to later occupational exploration and selection (Wise et al., 1976).

Another key idea in the goal was that children's career awareness is related to their sex and race. Boys in the elementary years, for example, express interest in three times as many occupations as girls the same age (Prediger et al., 1973). Also, whites display more knowledge about the rules of the social system and how to extract rewards from it than blacks, although their aspirations may be the same (Tomlinson and TenHouten, 1973). Based on these ideas, NIE set the goal of expanding children's pre-occupational and, secondarily, occupational interests and knowledge into areas that are nontraditional for their sex or race.

From the very beginning, the NIE staff saw television as central to the strategy for achieving this goal. An extensive review of the scholarly literature was commissioned to justify the choice of television, but it all resulted in two considerations. First, television seemed like a good way to reach many children; it pervades their home life and has started to make inroads into their school life with such successful educational series as *Electric Company* and *Inside Out*. Second, television not only gets the message through, but does so persuasively. *Sesame Street*, for example, had achieved measurable success in both cognitive and affective goal areas. Based on the considerations of pervasiveness and persuasiveness, NIE commissioned the development of a television series and supporting printed materials that could be both used by teachers in the classroom and viewed by children at home. Like *Sesame Street* and other successful educational series, this series was to be a synthesis of education and entertainment.

The example of *Sesame Street* also had an impact on NIE's plans for the way the series would be developed. Following the production model so successfully used by the Children's Television Workshop, educators, formative researchers, and television professionals were all to work together closely to produce the series (Land, 1971-1972; see also Lesser, 1974). First, the educators were to draw up a curriculum plan that would guide all later work, and then, in an intensive research and development phase, three experimental pilot television shows were to be produced and tested. Based on the lessons learned from the pilots, the series and supporting materials were to be designed, produced, and distributed. Finally, with the series complete and on the air, its effectiveness was to be assessed by independent summative evaluators. The series was, then, to be an educational experience not only for its audience, but also for those who seek to understand television and use it for prosocial ends.

THE *FREESTYLE* PROJECT

The *Freestyle* fundamentals were specified by NIE in a Request for Proposal (RFP). After the requisite bureaucratic and legal rituals of the proposal process, the contract to produce the series was awarded to a consortium that brought together the personnel and resources of six large and established television, and education, and research organizations in an ad hoc project. Like *Sesame Street, Freestyle* was created by top television professionals, educators, and researchers, but without the creation of a new organization. So *Freestyle* is also an experiment in adapting the *Sesame Street* production process to new and different organizational structures and constraints.

The television production component of the consortium was drawn from KCET, Community Television of Southern California, the Public Broadcasting Service affiliate in Los Angeles. An executive producer, hired specifically for the project, managed this component. He directed a small, permanent production staff and hired creative personnel such as script writers, directors, and musicians from the Hollywood talent pool on a short-term, as-needed basis. Technicians and other production personnel were drawn from the staff of the production house.

The curriculum planning component was located in the Office of the Los Angeles County Superintendent of Schools, a large organization with many consultants and planners on its staff. Responsibility for the development of a curriculum plan to guide all other work on the project was delegated to a small curriculum planning team of four people. The team employed several outside consultants for short periods, and also drew upon the resources of their own agency. In addition to curriculum planning, educational agency personnel were also responsible for developing teacher training materials for the series and assisting with the development of the printed materials.

The printed materials were the responsibility of Science Research Associates, an educational publisher. These materials included a teacher's guide and a student activities booklet for the series. The responsibility for the development of the materials was delegated to a project manager who employed freelance artists and writers from Los Angeles, New York, and Chicago.

The formative research component for the project was housed in the Annenberg School of Communication at the University of Southern California. The component included a principal investigator who was a faculty member of the university, several graduate student assistants for research design and test development, a data analyst, a field coordinator, and an administrative assistant. They were to conduct a number of research activities designed to improve both the entertainment value and educational effectiveness of the materials.

A community outreach unit, the smallest of the consortium components, was administered by the East Los Angeles College Foundation. The staff consisted, for the most part, of a field coordinator and a college administrator. While the television series and the print materials were intended for national distribution, this component's activities were limited to the Los Angeles area.

The sixth component, summative evaluation, was housed in the Institute for Social Research at the University of Michigan. This component was staffed by a principal investigator and two associates, along with a field coordinator. This permanent staff was supplemented by local coordinators in each of the research sites across the country and by the expertise and resources of persons at the Institute. The task of this component was to study both the development of *Freestyle* and its effects upon its audience. The results of these studies — that is to say, *our* studies — are the substance of this volume.

Each consortium component was represented by one or more of its staff members on the central planning and policy-making body called the core committee. This committee was to deal with consortium-wide policy and administrative issues and also to review the work of each component (except summative evaluation). The television production component was singled out for special attention in this regard. The committee was, for example, to examine scripts, segments of shows, and completed shows and either approve them or send them back for further work. The committee was also to direct the consortium toward resolution of any disagreements about the shows.

Two other groups played important roles in the project. A management council was composed of high-ranking administrators from several of the organizations that made up the consortium. This group's purpose was primarily to facilitate work on the project, but it also held the right of review and approval of the work. It did not, however, intervene in day-to-day operations. Finally, a review board composed of educators and community leaders from across the country was convened about twice a year to review and comment upon the work. Its authority, unlike the core committee and the management council, was largely moral authority, based on its collective experience and expertise.

These groups and individuals labored together for three years to develop *Freestyle*. What they did together is not easily or briefly summed up. *Freestyle* was planned, but it also evolved; it was created, but it was also negotiated and manufactured. The processes are all important because the strategy and materials directly reflect these processes. More than that, they *are* the processes which produced them. They are the creative solutions to problems, as well as the tough compromises struck in the course of organizational wrangling and the routine outputs of education and television organizations. The successes and failures of *Freestyle* in achieving its goal are, then, attributable to the development process and for this reason the evaluation begins with that process.

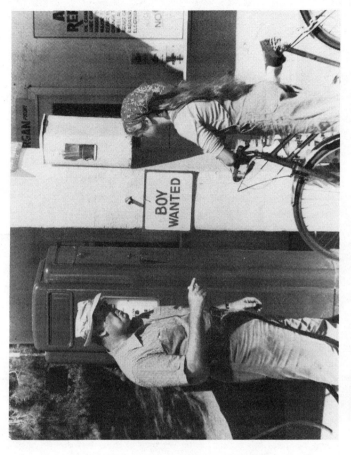

Chris assertively stakes a claim to Mat's job. *Photo by Melissa Trumbo*

Turned down by Mat, Chris pumps gas on her own to show Mat she can handle the job even though she's a girl. *Photo by Melissa Trumbo*

Chapter 2

CREATING THE SERIES

At some point in time projects such as *Freestyle* are only a vision. At first there are only a few basic concepts, a few general ideas, and a conviction that television can somehow be used to achieve an educational goal. The challenge is to fashion concrete products from these vague beginnings. *Freestyle,* we would argue, met the challenge with creative solutions. Thanks to its successes, and its failures too, the project offers some useful lessons to others who face the challenge of translating abstract goals and concepts into concrete media products.

The first lesson of *Freestyle* concerns not the effects of the series, but rather the process used to create it. Bringing together television professionals, educators, and researchers to accomplish the creative tasks does not by itself ensure success; a process must be fashioned which channels their respective contributions in a productive way. In the rest of this chapter we will examine how the creative process operated in the case of *Freestyle*.

It is simple enough to outline the steps by which *Freestyle* was developed. There were six of them:

(1) *Curriculum Planning.* The educators along with others in the consortium and outside consultants translated the goal of the project into a set of educational objectives (August to December 1976).

(2) *Pilot Design and Production.* The executive producer and other television professionals working together with the formative researchers and educators developed three experi-

mental pilot television shows (December 1976 to August 1977).

(3) *Curriculum Revision.* The educators with much assistance from a developmental psychologist extensively revised the original set of objectives (May to September 1977).

(4) *Pilot Testing.* The formative researchers tested the three pilots for appeal and comprehensibility and then the consortium chose one pilot as the prototype for the series (October to November 1977).

(5) *Series Design.* The executive producer, based on the results of the pilot testing, the advice of the researchers and educators and, of course, his own judgment developed the form and content of the series (November to December 1977).

(6) *Series Production.* The television professionals with some assistance from the educators and researchers wrote and produced the shows in the series (December 1977 to October 1978).

This brief listing of steps, of course, belies the complexity of the actual process. The educators did translate the goal into educational objectives, but the process was less one of scholarly deliberation upon the implications of the goal than one of tough, sometimes bitter, negotiations in which the curriculum was bargained out. Power within the project organization, as much as the merit of ideas, shaped the objectives. Television professionals working together with the educators and researchers did design and produce the shows, but the process was less one of engineering the shows from scientific theory and research than one of creating them within certain constraints. It was the educators and researchers who helped identify the constraints, but it was the television professionals — and the executive producer in particular — who actually created television shows that met these conditions. The intuition and judgement of the television professionals, more than the theory and research of the technical advisers, shaped the television series.

The first lesson to be learned from *Freestyle* comes down to this: Prosocial television can neither be deduced from scholarly literature nor engineered from scientific theory and research. Rather, it must be negotiated among those with an interest in the project and created by television professionals to meet conditions defined, in part, by educators and researchers. This lesson is the key to the rest. It teaches us that all the other lessons about the educational effectiveness of the *Freestyle* products cannot be used to deduce or engineer the form and content of future prosocial television series. At best they can help formulate the positions of those who must negotiate the content of the curriculum and inspire those who must create the form of the media materials. The history of *Freestyle* makes this quite clear.

PLANNING A CURRICULUM

The essentially political nature of curriculum planning was apparent from the very beginning of the project.[1] Curriculum planning was formally the responsibility of the educational agency which, in turn, had delegated the responsibility to a small curriculum planning team within the agency. While the team did the day-to-day work of collecting material and writing objectives, it shared the power to shape the form and content of the plan with the core committee, the management council, the funder, and even outside consultants. This, in turn, resulted in a planning process marked by tough negotiation and a plan marked by compromise.

Power and Politics: The Process

The dispersion of power within the consortium and beyond resulted, in part, from the right of the core committee, the management council, and the funder to review and approve the work of the curriculum planning team. However, other less formal organizational factors were also important. One such factor was that the team lacked expertise in a critical area of the proposed curriculum: sex-role development and stereotyping. This strange situation arose because the educational agency had classified the project as career education when developing the proposal. Following organizational routines, the educational agency assigned career education specialists to the curriculum planning team. While this may have been appropriate when the project was first organized, it became less so when the project moved away from traditional career education objectives (such as increasing knowledge of careers) and toward attempts to counter sociopsychological effects of sex-role stereotypes (such as changing males' negative attitudes about female leaders).

A second organizational factor that contributed to the dispersion of power throughout the consortium was the nature of the curriculum planning process itself. No real subject matter expertise or experience in the development of curricula was necessary to have a few common sense ideas about what stereotypes should be attacked or what knowledge and interests should be promoted. Because the techniques of curriculum planning are not very technical or esoteric, everybody involved in the project could have *some* idea for the plan. Because the curriculum planning team lacked critical expertise it also lacked the power to shape the plan which would have derived from having the best idea.

With power to shape the curriculum plan widely shared, important decicions about the plan were made through a legislative process in which those with a stake in the plan met as equals to discuss it and, when necessary, to negotiate its form and content. The forum for these discussions and negotiations was usually the meetings of the core committee. It convened regularly to review the progress of the curriculum planning team and to meet with the consultants who were hired to assist the team. In these sessions the reviewers could register their demands and make their cases. Sometimes the demands could be accommodated with minimal conflict, but when conflict did occur negotiation followed. After each review session the team expanded and revised the plan according to the demands presented and the compromises agreed upon. The curriculum planning process thus came to be structured as a series of cycles, each beginning with a review session and ending with the completion of a revised and expanded plan.

After nine major review-and-revision cycles a plan emerged consisting of a somewhat disorganized literature review and nine very general "experiential objectives." The objectives were:

(1) Children will practice behaviors such as independence and interdependence, and aggressiveness and yieldness (sic), depending upon the most appropriate behavior for the situation rather than on sex-role stereotyped behaviors.

(2) Children will experience a greater variety of work-related activities not previously considered appropriate for their sex roles.

(3) Children will experience situations that depict the limitations sex-role stereotyping has placed on both male and female choices and activities.

(4) Girls will experience situations that encourage them to take reasonable risks and not give up because of occasional failure.

(5) Children will experience situations that counteract the prevailing myth that females will be taken care of by males and will not need to be employed.

(6) Children will experience situations that encourage the development of positive attitudes toward girls in leadership roles.

(7) Girls will experience situations designed to help them attribute their successes to ability, not solely to luck.

(8) Girls will experience situations designed to evoke and reward appropriate degrees of independence, initiative, and self-direction.

(9) Boys will experience situations that evoke and reward nurturant behavior.

Key Compromises: Form and Content of the Plan

These nine objectives are quite different from the final version of the curriculum plan yet they are of interest for several reasons. For one, they contain the germ of the ideas eventually realized as the three content themes of the completed *Freestyle* curriculum. The content theme of adult work and family roles, for example, is implicit in the mention of "the limitations sex-role stereotyping has placed on both male and female choices" (objective 3) and "the prevailing myth that females will be taken care of by males" (objective 5). The theme of pre-occupational activities is suggested in the mention of "work-related activities" (objective 2), and the theme of behavioral skills is clearly present in the mention of "independence" (objective 1), "reasonable risks" (objective 4), and "leadership" (objective 6). The messages of *Freestyle* are, then, an elaboration of the ideas only vaguely formulated in the first curriculum plan.

Another reason this plan is of interest is that its form and content clearly reflect the process that produced them. In terms of *form,* the objectives were merely statements requiring children to be presented with some vaguely defined experience. Beyond the general requirement that these experiences promote some desirable attitude or behavior (such as risk-taking or nurturance), the content of these experiences was not specified. This nonspecific form of the objectives may be traced to the review-and-revision process that was more conducive to enumerating general ideas than spelling out specific messages. The time for discussion and debate among the curriculum planning team, the reviewers, and the consultants was very limited; it was sufficient only to agree upon generalities, leaving the ill-equipped team to struggle with specifics later. Further, as in any political process, compromise was often facilitated when issues were left in vague terms.

In terms of *content,* the objectives were the result of discussion, negotiation, and compromise on a variety of issues. One content issue was the notion of an "experiential objective."

This concept had been introduced to the curriculum planning team by a consultant who argued that traditional outcome or performance objectives were better suited to curricula seeking cognitive change, for example, learning of new material. He proposed experiential objectives as as alternative more suited to a curriculum seeking long-term affective change. He defined these objectives as descriptions of the experiences to be provided for children in the television shows and the class discussions rather than a specification of the expected outcome of these experiences.

The curriculum planning team was enthusiastic about experiential objectives though others in the consortium were not. The formative researchers, in particular, objected to them. They argued that if they were to test the shows, they wanted to know what to test for. The curriculum planning team, however, prevailed on this issue, due in part to their argument that experiences rather than learner outcomes were the language of the television professionals who would use the plan.

Another content issue was the treatment of racial and ethnic stereotyping. According to the project goal, this was to be an important concern of the project. As the project got underway, however, the funder's project officer intervened in an attempt to reduce the importance of the topic. This aroused a good deal of consternation among the multiracial review board and several components of the consortium. This issue was bitterly debated and contributed to several resignations from the project. A compromise was long in coming, but eventually the idea of treating ethnicity as it "interacts" with sex-role stereotyping was worked out. No experiential objectives dealing with this interaction were produced, however.

Still another content issue was much less bitterly debated, but had a greater impact on the content of the plan. This issue was nothing less than how the project's goal should be interpreted. The funder's original goal for the project had been to expand career awareness by increasing children's awareness of, and interest in, those childhood activities and adult occupa-

tions that are nontraditional for their sex. Several consultants
to the curriculum planning team argued, however, that expanding interests was much less important than countering certain
psychosocial effects of sex-role stereotyping. These effects
included women's fear of risk-taking, lack of independence,
and their propensity to attribute success to luck rather than
effort and ability. They also included men's limited nurturing
skills and negative attitudes toward women in leadership roles.
The consultants portrayed expanding interests and countering
stereotypes as two separate and competing interpretations of
the goal.

The consultants were particularly compelling because in
their arguments they provided interesting and research-
documented content ideas while the team's own work was not
producing many such ideas. The consultants' point of view
prevailed and their ideas for countering sex-role stereotypes
became the content of most of the experiential objectives push-
ing aside ideas about expanding interests in activities and occupations. As one member of the curriculum planning team put it,
the curriculum was about sex-role stereotypes and not career
awareness.

In this way, outside consultants, who were powerful because they had ideas when ideas were badly needed, changed
the course of curriculum planning. It was the ideas of the
consultants which were later collected into the behavioral skills
content theme and, in turn, became the "figure" or primary
dramatic content of most *Freestyle* episodes. These ideas, as
we will discuss in later chapters, also provided the project with
its most difficult communication task. The *Freestyle* messages
about these ideas were not always understood by children and
often had little impact on them (see Chapters 3 and 5 in this
volume). There is irony here: These ideas, which were essentially grafted onto the original goal in the course of organizational politics, gave *Freestyle* both its dramatic heart and its
greatest difficulties.

DEVELOPING THREE PILOTS

The development process for the three experimental pilot television shows provides a marked contrast to that for the curriculum plan. Production of the pilots, and later the series, was the responsibility of the television production component within the consortium. This responsibility was, in turn, delegated to the executive producer. Like the curriculum planning team, the executive producer was to submit his work to the consortum's core committee and management council for review. Unlike the curriculum planning team, however, the executive producer did not really have to share the power to shape the shows with others. He, not the core committee, was the final authority on all matters pertaining to the shows. In short, he was the creator of *Freestyle*.

Creativity and Constraint: The Process

The power of the executive producer rested simply, but effectively, on his greater ability to solve the problems of creating television for which there was no ready model or formula. The executive producer, a seven-year veteran of the Children's Television Workshop, was hired because of his expertise in the production of quality educational television. He, in turn, commissioned top Hollywood television professionals to script and direct the shows. The executive producer was, then, able to face the creative challenges presented by *Freestyle* with a team of high-powered television talent.

The others in the consortium — the educators and researchers — were included in the project because they too were experts. Their educational experience and research skills were to guide the work of the television professionals. However, their ability to do so was limited by the state of the art in educational planning and formative research. The educators and researchers simply could not provide the unequivocal and precise advice necessary to effectively determine production decisions. The executive producer was often required to rely upon his intuition and judgment as a television professional in making production decisions. Thus, the elaborate plans for review of the executive producer's work by the core committee became pointless. Power over the television shows remained firmly in the hands of the executive producer.

Still, the contribution of the educators and researchers to the *Freestyle* shows and strategy was significant. They served as personal advisers to the executive producer who called on them at specific points in the television production process. Reasonably enough, these points occurred when the process required the executive producer to make important production decisions. These "decision points" included the design of formats for the three experimental pilots, the choice and improvement of scripts for the pilots, the choice of one of the pilots as a prototype for the series, the design of the series, and the development of the series scripts. At these points, the advisers could interpret the curriculum plan, present needs of teachers and other users of the project's products, provide data on the interests and preferences of children, and, in general, formulate and reinforce all the problems and constraints the executive producer and his staff had to solve or consider in developing the shows. These decision points are, then, the key points at which the *Freestyle* strategy and materials took shape.

Pilot Formats

The first decision point in the development of the *Freestyle* strategy was the design of formats for the three experimental pilot television shows. Early in the project it had been decided that a different format would be developed for each of the three pilots and the pilot that proved to be the most effective would be chosen as the prototype for the series. The opportunity to produce three very different shows gave the executive producer and his advisers a good deal of creative freedom, but there were also some important constraints.

One constraint was that the educational messages had to be presented in a way that would hold the interest of children. The shows had to be more than a vehicle for the messages; they had to be good entertainment for 9- to 12-year-olds, particularly if they were to attract an audience of home viewers. A second, more specific constraint was that the shows had to be half an hour in length for afternoon or evening broadcast into homes, but each half-hour show had to be divisible into two quarter-hour segments for daytime broadcast into schools. This constraint was imposed by the educational advisers. They found that teachers preferred quarter-hour programs. With the warm-up, viewing, and follow-up activities this resulted in a lesson of about 45 minutes duration — a common length for upper elementary school. They also found that the instructional program schedules of many educational broadcasters were structured around quarter-hour programs.

The executive producer's solution to the creative problem of designing pilots that fit these constraints was to borrow the short segment format of *Sesame Street*. The first of the three pilots was a cross between *Sesame Street* and an adult variety show. A troupe of young performers along with a guest star performed several musical numbers and comic sketches that introduced and tied together animated and filmed segments. Each of these sketches and segments addressed one or more of the educational objectives and the segment in the middle of the half hour could be removed to divide the show into two quarter-hour segments. This was called the bridge segment.

The second pilot also employed the short segment format, but was more story-like. Each of the segments followed the adventures of four youngsters through various settings. Music and comedy remained important elements, but the slightly longer and more realistic segments gave the show more continuity and coherence. Here again, each segment addressed one or more objectives and a bridge segment united the two quarter-hours into a single show.

The executive producer's rationale for his choice of the short segment format was well developed. First, this format could both entertain and educate its audience as evidenced by the success of *Sesame Street*. Second, this format could most effectively meet the condition that each half hour be divisible into quarter-hour shows because the short segments offered natural division points within the show. Third, the short segments could be used several times during the run of the series, thus amortizing their cost over several shows. Finally, those segments which research showed to be low in either educational or entertaiment value could be eliminated without losing the entire show.

The educators and researchers were not completely convinced, however. The formative researchers were concerned about the entertainment value of the short segment format. Research showed that 9- to 12-year-olds were more interested in narrative formats (for example, sit-coms and action/adventure) than in short segment shows (for example, variety). The educators, on the other hand, were concerned about the educational acceptability of the format. They argued, first, that the short segment format did not allow the in-depth treatment of characters, problems, and solutions appropriate both to the interests of 9- to 12-year-olds and to the affective content of the curriculum. Second, teachers who might view entertainment and education as antithetical would see the music and comedy of the short segment format as a waste of precious class time. Finally, a large number of short segments in a show, particularly if each segment dealt with a different educational objective, made the organization of a coherent lesson around each show very difficult.

While the educators did not argue that the short segment format should be dropped, they did press the executive producer for a format in which one or two topics would be explored in depth. The executive producer responded that a show with a narrative format, divisible into two separate and complete shows, presented creative problems. At one point he suggested producing a narrative show in only the half-hour version. Later he suggested dropping the third pilot altogether, using the money saved to improve the other two pilots, The educators persisted, however, and finally the executive producer agreed to attempt a show that would meet their demands.

Here again, as at so many other points in the development of *Freestyle,* there is irony. The executive producer was very reluctant to develop a narrative format, but finally succumbed to pressure. In so doing he created what would later come to be the key to the entire *Freestyle* television strategy. The show he designed was something like a two-part soap opera. The first quarter hour had a cliffhanger ending and the second resolved the dilemma. This cliffhanger device allowed the show to be divided into two parts yet retain narrative continuity — and children's interest. The device did not, however, meet the condition that the quarter-hour shows be able to stand completely alone as the educators had originally desired. Still, everyone agreed that the design was an adequate solution to the creative problem.

Premises

With a basic format for each of the pilots, the executive producer set to work devising premises or story ideas. These premises addressed one or more of the experiential objectives then in use and were to be used by the writers as the basis of their scripts. The premises were, then, to be the bridge between the work of the curriculum planners and the work of the television script writers.

Rather than building a bridge, however, the executive producer found he had, in his words, "to leap the chasm" between the general ideas of the experiential objectives and the more specific premise ideas. The original curriculum plan simply did not provide the material necessary for bridge building. The

executive producer was required to generate premises for
scripts that would, for example, promote female leadership and
male nurturance. But he was given no information about the
specific attitudes, behaviors, or personality traits that underlie
these concepts.

Accordingly, the executive producer and the writers used
their own common-sense notions about these concepts. It is
not surprising that at times they failed. For example, an animated female character in the first pilot was intended to promote female leadership. But the formative researchers found
that she was perceived, especially by boys, not as a leader, but
as a smart-alecy and bossy girl. For the second pilot the executive producer commissioned a segment on male nurturance in
which a hispanic boy and his father cook together in the
mother's absence. He and the writers soon found, however,
that their thinking about nurturance was so unfocused that they
redefined the purpose of the segment. Instead of being about
nurturance, they said it was a segment about cooking as a
nontraditional activity for Hispanic males. Later, in reviewing
the script a member of the Hispanic community argued that
males cooking in such a situation would hardly be a nontraditional activity for Hispanics or anyone else. And still later
when the segment had been taped, another member of the
Hispanic community argued that the father-son relationship
depicted was more informal than was common in Hispanic
families and that presenting it as a superior model was a value
judgment that could certainly be debated.

In other segments, the common-sense notions of the executive producer and writers were not so much wrong as trivial. In
one segment, for example, nurturance was equated with being
nice to the dog and in another risk-taking was portrayed as a girl
asking a boy to dance. The adult occupations shown in very
brief film clips in the first pilot included a female construction
worker and a male nurse. These occupations, it was pointed
out by a member of the core committee, are indeed nontradi-

tional; so nontraditional, in fact, that they are *stereotypes* of nontraditional occupations.

By the time the executive producer began work on the third pilot, however, some of the problems and shortcomings of the first two pilots had become clear to him. A number of the completed segments from the first pilot had been tested on children for comprehension and appeal and it was clear that some of the messages were misunderstood. Also, critiques of the core committee and others had been digested. As one member of core told the executive producer, some of the short segments were too much like public service announcements: cute perhaps, but not very deep.

With this in mind, the executive producer chose several objectives he felt had been inadequately addressed in the first two pilots. Nurturance could be given some meaning and substance beyond simply being nice. Risk-taking could be shown as an important component of success in career-related activities. Also, nontraditional childhood activities should be taken more seriously. Building upon these objectives, he developed a premise for a half-hour dramatic show revolving around the "sorcerer's apprentice" theme. A young girl, very interested in auto mechanics, seeks a summer job in a service station. In so doing she risks the disapproval of her friends and the insults of the crusty old owner. She gets the job, but soon takes an unreasonable risk by attempting a complex auto repair without sufficient training. Disaster ensues, but the station's young mechanic notices her interest in cars is serious and begins to train her in mechanics. Later, when an emergency occurs the girl is able to save the day. This premise, then, distinguished risks taken without sufficient ability or knowledge from more reasonable risks. It also presented a male whose nurturing behavior included teaching as well as simply being nice. And it offered a glimpse of auto mechanics. More importantly this premise brought to life Chris, the young sorcerer's apprentice, who would eventually be the model for all those created to live in the world of *Freestyle*. Her adventures would be the prototype for all those to follow. This pilot was the genesis for the world of *Freestyle*.

Scripts

The premises for all three pilots were turned over to teams of writers drawn from the Hollywood talent pool. As draft scripts were completed they were returned to the executive producer who again called upon his advisers. The educators and researchers provided open-ended, unstructured critiques of the scripts which the executive producer called his "theater reviews." In addition, the researchers organized small groups of teachers and parents who rated the scripts for comprehensibility and interest to 9- to 12-year-olds. The reviews and ratings helped the executive producer cull out "sure losers" among the short segment scripts for the first and second pilots and spot problems with the storyline and characters in the third pilot. The advisers were thus successful in helping the executive producer steer clear of material that was unacceptable to teachers or minority groups or material that was just plain dull.

While the advisers were often very successful in telling the executive producer what *not* to do, they were less successful in telling him what he should do. Their ratings and reviews were usually too equivocal to accept as guarantee of a successful script and too vague to serve as instructions for improvement of a weak script. Here, as at other decision points, the advisers did not determine the decisions of the executive producer, but did help to establish some of the constraints (that is, the acceptability of the material to its various users) within which decisions had to be made.

The executive producer digested the counsel of his advisers and used it as he saw fit in making suggestions to the writers for script revisions. As is traditional in Hollywood, the scripts passed through a number of revisions before being taped or filmed. The advisers played only a very limited role in the later script revisions or in the actual production of the scripts. It was still necessary to choose among the three pilots, however, and the advisers turn would come again.

REVISING THE CURRICULUM PLAN

The first curriculum plan served the project through the production of the three experimental pilot television shows, but not without a good deal of criticism. The consortium was then forced to reopen negotiations on the curriculum plan.

Building a Consensus

The executive producer, in particular, was an early and harsh critic of the original curriculum plan. He pointed out that lack of conceptual guidance had resulted in several expensive mistakes during the scripting and production of the pilots. He argued that the plan was too vague to guide the development of an entire television series. And he faulted the use of experiential objectives instead of learner outcomes with aiding and abetting this vagueness.

Others in the project joined the executive producer to criticize the plan as dwelling too much on the "crippling effects of stereotyping" without offering positive alternatives. Some criticized the plan's lack of attention to the problems encountered by boys as a result of sex-role stereotypes. Still others were concerned that the television series would not find a place in the crowded elementary curriculum without plans for "infusing" the lessons and materials into other areas of the curriculum. These criticisms were voiced not only by the project staff, but also by several school administrators and teachers who had been approached to help in testing the pilot television shows.

Drawing upon all these criticisms, a member of the curriculum planning team assembled a list of proposed changes:

- The basic idea in each of the experiential objectives (e.g., male nurturance, female risk-taking) should be retained, but specific

and detailed information about them must be included in a
revised curriculum plan.

- Material addressing the needs and problems of boys and setting
  a more positive tone should be included in a revised plan.

- The experiential objectives should be replaced with learner
  outcome objectives.

- Both cognitive and affective outcomes should be specified.

- Curriculum infusion strategies should be developed.

The movement for curriculum change immediately encountered resistance, however. Some members of the curriculum
planning team, recalling the long and sometimes bitter debates
that shaped the first plan, were reluctant to begin the process
again. They were, however, persuaded to try when it was
agreed that the content of the original plan could serve as the
basis for the revised plan.

After some behind the scenes arm twisting, disagreement
remained on only one issue: the form of the objectives. Some of
the educational agency staff members argued that if the objectives of the project were translated from experiential into
learner outcome objectives, at least some of them would require changed attitudes among children. Attitude change would
be difficult to achieve, they argued, and the project would be
stigmatized as a failure. The formative researchers responded,
however, that if specific attitudes were singled out for attention
and equally specific messages were aimed at them, then attitude change was possible. Others joined with the formative
researchers to argue that, in any case, the use of outcome
objectives would facilitate the development of specific messages by the curriculum planners. They warned that if the
curriculum planners did not specify the messages themselves
then, by default, the script writers would become the real
curriculum planners. This last argument was decisive and consensus on the general form and content of the revised curriculum was finally achieved.

Coming to terms with the need for curriculum revision was much less of an ordeal for the consortium than the earlier curriculum planning phase had been, but it was no less an excercise in organizational politics. The original curriculum plan had been skillfully used to build a consensus that a revision could and should be undertaken; then arguments for the various proposed additions and changes had been compellingly presented by those advocating them. The executive producer, for example, needed "specifics" to facilitate his own work and he made a case for them using some carefully selected anecdotes concerning mistakes made during production of the pilots. He and his supporters also managed to tie the idea of greater specificity to the idea of outcome objectives and to sell both to the consortium as a package deal. Similarly, others in the project sold their interpretations of comments made by a few school teachers and administrators as prerequisites for user acceptance of the project's materials. The teachers' and administrators' ideas of more attention to the needs of boys and a more positive tone had previously been proposed by educators within the project, but the comments of the small sample of potential users allowed the staff members to legitimate and press their case. Organizational politics had not, then, disappeared from the project, but it had become a good deal more sophisticated.

Three Content Themes Emerge

Consensus on the need for a curriculum revision was achieved only a few months before production of the full television series was scheduled to begin. The consortium concluded that it needed help. A developmental psychologist whose work was widely respected within the consortium was commissioned to provide the sorely needed "specifics." Within a few weeks of being commissioned the psychologist presented to the consortium the single most important document in the development of the *Freestyle* strategy. In it she organized the ideas scattered throughout the original curriculum into three content themes — behavioral skills, nontraditional interests and activities, and adult work and family roles. The ideas of leadership, risk-taking, and the like were collected into a theme which the document labeled "behavioral skills" to suggest that such behaviors are not immutable personality traits, but rather skills that can be developed. Independence, assertiveness, initiative and self-direction, striving for competence and risking failure and, of course, leadership were listed as the skills to be emphasized for girls. Those to be emphasized for boys were emotional expressiveness, sensitivity to other's feelings and perspectives, nurturance and helping others and, finally, cooperation. All of the skills for girls were drawn from or suggested by the original curriculum plan, as were nurturance and helping for boys. Cooperation and other skills for boys were included in an effort to balance out the heavy emphasis on girls in the original plan.

The document went on to provide a general definition of each of these behaviors as well as to detail a number of specific steps that comprised the skills. For example, a strategy for attaining a leadership position was outlined along with "goal-related" and "people-related" skills for exercising effective leadership once the position was attained.

The idea of nontraditional work-related activities — or "pre-occupational interests and activities" as the funder called them — was developed into the second theme. Noting research on the relationship between pre-occupational interests and activities and later career choice, the document singled out several categories of interests and activities for attention. For girls these were mechanical activities and spatial relationships (for example, electronics and use of tools and plans), athletics, mathematics, science, and traditionally masculine household jobs. For boys they were artistic activities, writing and skill with words, social service activities, child care, and traditionally feminine household tasks. In each of these categories a number of specific interests and activities were listed. This theme thus returned to the funder's original intention of focusing on the promotion of non-stereotyped interests and activities that relate to adult work and family roles.

The third theme was nontraditional work and family roles. Noting that traditional sex roles restrict options of both men and women, the document outlined messages for each sex. The messages for girls focused on the increasing economic importance for women to develop careers outside the home, as well as the noneconomic rewards of such careers. The messages for boys focused on the rewards of expanded child care roles for men and the importance of facilitating wives' careers. A message for both sexes suggested that both men and women can certainly do household tasks that are nontraditional for their sex. In addition to these messages, the document suggested that children be exposed to a variety of jobs stereotyped in the past, and to the idea that sex and ethnicity do not affect qualifications for those jobs.

The document went on to point out how these themes complemented each other and how they could be combined in the television shows — and in children's lives. Behavioral skills, the document noted, describe *how* people relate to their world; the interests and activities describe *what* they do. A girl could, for example, assert herself while trying a new and nontraditional activity such as mechanics. The executive producer later called this idea the "figure/ground relationship" and used it as the basis for plotting each of the series' episodes

The development of the three content themes fulfilled the psychologist's commission to provide the long-sought "specifics" for the revised plan. The document was indeed a rich source of information which could be used to develop the revised curriculum plan and, later, messages for each episode in the series. It also provided a positive tone for the curriculum with its emphasis on developing behavioral skill and increasing pre-occupational interests. At the same time it suggested how such career education concepts as pre-occupational activities and the effects of sex-role stereotyping could be treated as complementary rather than competing interpretations of the project goal. This document provided the transition from the vague concepts in the original curriculum plan to a much more precise and detailed revised plan. In short, this document provided the content of *Freestyle's* curriculum, though not the final form of its curriculum plan.

Manufacturing Objectives

With the developmental psychologist's document in hand, the entire consortium assembled at a planning retreat to begin the process of putting the revised curriculum plan into its final form. The primary task, as the consortium saw it, was to produce performance or outcome objectives drawing upon both the original experiential objectives and the developmental psychologist's document. The work routine to accomplish this task was based on three rules which were never explicitly formulated, but which nevertheless promoted orderly manufacture of the objectives. One rule was that outcome objectives should be developed from each of the experiential objectives in the original curriculum plan. Specifically, each experiential objective was to be restated as a subgoal and then a number of objectives relevant to the subgoal were to be written. A second rule was that the set of outcome objectives developed from each of the experiential objectives should include cognitive, affective and, if appropriate, behavioral outcomes. A third rule was that, whenever possible, the substance of the objective should be drawn from the developmental psychologist's document. The document proved to be so successful at inspiring ideas for the objectives that it soon came to be called, only slightly facetiously, "the gospel."

The use of these three rules to generate objectives is exemplified by the work on the original experiential objective dealing with risk-taking. This objective stated:

Girls will experience situations that encourage them to take reasonable risks and not give up because of occasional failure.

First, the objective was restated as this subgoal:

Children will strive for competence by taking reasonable risks and learning how to cope with failure.

'Next, objectives were generated for the subgoal. Those objectives dealing with the concept of reasonable risk-taking included:

4.1 When given a choice of tasks, the child will be able to identify the reasonable (50-50 chance of success) risk and make an action choice.

4.1.1 More children will be able to define the difference between reasonable and unreasonable (or no) risks and difference between success and failure.

4.1.2 Children will demonstrate increased preferences for reasonable risk-taking.

4.1.3 Some children will demonstrate reasonable risk-taking behavior.

In these objectives the operation of the rule that the key concept of the original objective (i.e., risk-taking) be developed into a set of outcome objectives may be clearly seen. So too is the operation of the rule that cognitive, affective and, if appropiate, behavioral outcomes be specified. Finally, the operation of the rule that the substance of the objectives should be drawn from the developmental psychologist's document is also clear when the objectives above are compared to the relevant section of that document:

4. Striving for competence and risking failure.

Definition: Achievement motivation is the desire to do well or to gain competence in situations where standards of excellence apply. It is most adaptive when not accompanied by high fear of failure.

A. Reasonable risk-taking. Selecting and working hardest on tasks with a moderate probability of success (i.e., ones where you think you have about a 50-50 chance of success). Either very easy or very hard tasks get less effort.

After the development of a few such objectives the consortium agreed that this was indeed the correct approach to the task. At the conclusion of the planning retreat the consortium commissioned the curriculum planning team to complete the plan. The team continued the routine of developing subgoals and outcome objectives from each of the experiential objectives. It also continued to use the cognition-affect-behavior taxonomy and the material from the psychologist's document. So central, in fact, was the material from the document to the content of the objectives that the team developed a graphic format for presentation of the revised plan that juxtaposed objectives with the section of the document from which they were drawn. Large sections of the document were thus inserted into the revised plan with only minor editing and additions. Only a week after the planning retreat the team produced a draft of the revised curriculum plan. The nine original experiential objectives had been restated as eight subgoals. (Figure 2.1 shows the original objectives in column 1 and the subgoals into which they first evolved in column 2.) Most of the subgoals were simple and direct restatements of the original objective though several, such as objective 5, were more extensively reworked using ideas from the developmental psychologist's document. A cooperation subgoal was also added.

Over the next month the subgoals and objectives continued to evolve (as shown in column 3 of Figure 2.1). One change was the consolidation of several subgoals, reducing their number to six. Another change was reflected in the wording of the nurturance subgoal. As the change in wording suggests, outcome objectives requiring children to actually display such skills as emotional expressiveness and nurturance were dropped in favor of objectives merely requiring children to identify these skills in others. A number of objectives requiring behavioral outcomes were dropped from other subgoals as well. These objectives were eliminated after discussions with the formative researchers who argued that behavioral change in many cases would be an unrealistic expectation. A third change, not di-

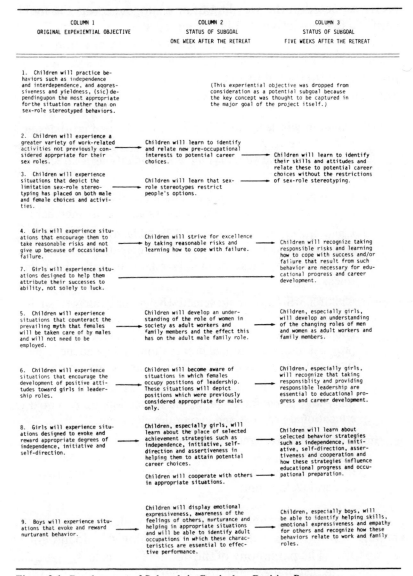

COLUMN 1 ORIGINAL EXPERIENTIAL OBJECTIVE	COLUMN 2 STATUS OF SUBGOAL ONE WEEK AFTER THE RETREAT	COLUMN 3 STATUS OF SUBGOAL FIVE WEEKS AFTER THE RETREAT
1. Children will practice behaviors such as independence and interdependence, and aggressiveness and yieldness, (sic) depending upon the most appropriate for the situation rather than on sex-role stereotyped behaviors.	(This experiential objective was dropped from consideration as a potential subgoal because the key concept was thought to be captured in the major goal of the project itself.)	
2. Children will experience a greater variety of work-related activities not previously considered apprpriate for their sex roles.	Children will learn to identify and relate new pre-occupational interests to potential career choices.	Children will learn to identify their skills and attitudes and relate these to potential career choices without the restrictions of sex-role stereotyping.
3. Children will experience situations that depict the limitation sex-role stereotyping has placed on both male and female choices and activities.	Children will learn that sex-role stereotypes restrict people's options.	
4. Girls will experience situations that encourage them to take reasonable risks and not give up because of occasional failure.	Children will strive for excellence by taking reasonable risks and learning how to cope with failure.	Children will recognize taking responsible risks and learning how to cope with success and/or failure that result from such behavior are necessary for educational progress and career development.
7. Girls will experience situations designed to help them attribute their successes to ability, not solely to luck.		
5. Children will experience situations that counteract the prevailing myth that females will be taken care of by males and will not need to be employed.	Children will develop an understanding of the role of women in society as adult workers and family members and the effect this has on the adult male family role.	Children, especially girls, will develop an understanding of the changing roles of men and women as adult workers and family members.
6. Children will experience situations that encourage the development of positive attitudes toward girls in leadership roles.	Children will become aware of situations in which females occupy positions of leadership. These situations will depict positions which were previously considered appropriate for males only.	Children, especially girls, will recognize that taking responsiblity and providing responsible leadership are essential to educational progress and career development.
8. Girls will experience situations designed to evoke and reward appropriate degrees of independence, initiative and self-direction.	Children, especially girls, will learn about the place of selected achievement strategies such as independence, initiative, self-direction and assertiveness in helping them to attain potential career choices.	Children will learn about selected behavior strategies such as independence, initiative, self-direction, assertiveness and cooperation and how these strategies influence educational progress and occupational preparation.
	Children will cooperate with others in appropriate situations.	
9. Boys will experience situations that evoke and reward nurturant behavior.	Children will display emotional expressiveness, awareness of the feelings of others, nurturance and helping in appropriate situations and will be able to identify adult occupations in which these characteristics are essential to effective performance.	Children, especially boys, will be able to identify helping skills, emotional expressiveness and empathy for others and recognize how these behaviors relate to work and family roles.

Figure 2.1 Development of Subgoals in Curriculum Revision Process

rectly reflected in the wording of any subgoals, was the inclusion of a few objectives explicitly aimed at ethnic groups. These were intended to capture the concept of the interaction of sex roles and ethnicity. At this point the six subgoals closely approximated their final form though they were modified slightly after discussions with the funder. At last they were complete:

(1) Children will learn to identify their skills and attitudes and relate these to potential career choices without the restrictions of sex-role stereotyping and ethnicity as it affects sex-role stereotyping.

(2) Children will develop an understanding of the changing roles of men and women as adult workers and family members.

(3) Children, especially boys, will be able to identify helping skills, emotional expressiveness, and empathy for others and recognize how these behaviors relate to work and family roles.

(4) Children will learn about selected behavior strategies, such as independence, initiative, self-direction, assertiveness, and cooperation and how these strategies influence educational progress and occupational preparation. Independence, initiative, and self-direction are especially important for girls.

(5) Children, especially girls, will recognize that taking responsibility and providing responsibile leadership are essential to educational progress and career development.

(6) Children will recognize that taking reasonable risks and learning how to cope with the success and / or failure that results from taking risks are necessary for educational progress and career development.

In its final form the curriculum plan included most of the material from the developmental psychologist's document in some form. The parsimony of the document was lost, however, because the original experiential objectives, and not the three content themes, were routinely used to develop the subgoals and objectives. This routine expedited the task, but lost the themes among 6 subgoals and 84 objectives. (See Appendix B for complete list of subgoals and objectives.) The themes were not lost forever, of course, and once again the irony of events demand comment.

The executive producer would later rediscover the three themes when searching for a way to organize the complex curriculum plan into specific messages for the series. The themes would become his primary planning tool in allocating specific messages to various episodes. Further, the developmental psychologist's discussion of the particular preoccupational activities, behavioral skills, and adult roles would become his source of the messages themselves. The subgoals and objectives — so long in coming — would be of only limited use to him in these tasks.

TESTING THE PILOTS

The completion of the revised curriculum plan established the most basic constraint within which the series would have to be created — the content. Soon after, another constraint was established — the format. This was to have been determined by the activities of the formative researchers, but as it turned out other factors were influential as well — most significantly, the ideas of the executive producer. Here again the executive producer excercised his role of creator while the formative researchers served as his advisers.

The Research

While the attention of the educators had been focused on the curriculum revision, the formative researchers had planned and executed their testing of the pilot television shows. More than 1600 fourth, fifth, and sixth graders and their teachers in four cities had participated in a research project designed to help choose among the format alternatives presented by the three pilots. The alternative presented by the first pilot was to provide an explicit lesson or moral in each of the short segments. The cast sang and danced about stereotypes in the first segment; they defined, explained, and illustrated stereotypes in later segments; and they sang and danced about the eventual elimination of stereotypes in the concluding segment. In contrast, the alternative presented by the third pilot was to tell a single coherent story modeling desirable behaviors and activities. Risk-taking, nurturance, and mechanical interest and ability were all part of the story, but were not explicitly discussed in the show. The choice was, in short, lessons versus models with the second pilot offering a compromise between the two.

The research was designed around three criteria for choosing among the alternatives: acceptability to teachers of each of the alternatives, entertainment value or appeal to students, and comprehensibility to students. To assess acceptability to teachers and appeal to students the three pilots were compared on several rating scales completed by teachers and their students. To assess comprehensibility they were compared on a number of questions designed to gauge children's understanding of both the plot and the messages. In addition, the comprehensibility of the various experiential objectives was compared by grouping the message comprehension measures according to the objective they dealt with, rather that the pilot in which they were presented. Finally, the contribution of the printed materials was assessed by comparing the understanding of children who had only viewed the shows to those who had supplemented viewing with discussions and activities suggested in the printed materials.

The formative researchers made no attempt to measure attitude change or other impacts of the pilots. They maintained, first of all, that the experiential objectives from which the pilots were developed required evaluators to determine if children really had the specified experience, not if they were changed by it. They acknowledged, however, that this argument was something of a technicality. They also maintained that impact of only three rather unrelated shows would probably be quite limited, and the attempt to measure it would not yield useful information. Impact on children was, then, not a criterion used to assess the merits of the different pilots.

The results of the pilot research were eagerly awaited by the consortium. But educational acceptability, entertainment value, and comprehensibility were not the only criteria for making the choice. Cost was also a consideration. The three pilots had ranged in cost from about $84,000 for the third pilot with its dramatic format to about $188,000 for the first pilot with its short segment format. Even the figure of $84,000 was more than double the amount budgeted for each show. The executive producer had anticipated the inadequacy of the original budget for the series while producing the pilots. In a masterful display of grantsmanship he convinced the funder both to increase the budget substantially and to cut the number of shows in the series from 26 to 13. Further, two of the pilots were to be used as a part of the 13-episode series, thus requiring production of only 11 new shows. Even with these adjustments the executive producer maintained that the budget was still not adequate to produce a series of variety shows similar to the first pilot. He warned that if the data clearly supported the first pilot as the prototype for the series, then the series would have fewer cartoons and films per show and that these would have to be reused more often than desired. If the test results clearly called for a variety show format he could do something like the classic kid's show of the 1950s, *Mickey Mouse Club*.

Another *Mickey Mouse Club* was, however, clearly not the executive producer's preferred alternative. Even though the formative researchers had put pressure on him to remain undecided until the test results were in, the executive producer had a clear preference among the three pilots. And he had a good deal of difficulty in keeping it a secret. In an interview with a television columnist conducted before the research had even begun, he was quoted as saying that the third pilot was the most effective because 9- to 12-year-olds like stories and respond to role models. He hastened to add, however, that all three pilots would be tested and a decision on the format would be made when the results were available. The columnist himself found the first pilot "decidedly instructional in tone" while the third "engagingly played." Others, both within and outside of the consortium, reinforced the producer's judgment. It is not surprising, then, that the producer commissioned a script for a dramatic episode before the researchers' data were available and developed the premise for still another.

The Results

A potentially fascinating exercise in organizational politics was avoided when the researchers released their data and conclusions. The data on educational acceptability and entertainment value showed the third pilot to be the overwhelming choice of both students and their teachers. Students' understanding of the plot of the third pilot was also the highest of the three; however, students' comprehension of the message was significantly lower than for the other two. Despite this last finding the researchers gave the go-ahead to use the third pilot as the prototype for the series.

The objective-by-objective analysis of message comprehension shed light on the poor showing of the third pilot in regard to message comprehension. In general, those messages about behavioral skills were less well understood than those about nontraditional jobs and activities. This was particularly true of the third pilot. Its messages about risk-taking and nurturance were less well understood than its message about auto mechanics as a nontraditional activity for girls. Here was the first indication that behavioral skills would pose a particularly difficult communication task.

Based on these results the researchers argued that those messages most explicitly presented were best comprehended. They suggested that while some messages (that is, those about the concrete nontraditional interests, activities, and jobs) lend themselves to more explicit portrayal than others (that is, those about the more abstract behavioral skills), steps must be taken to make all messages explicit. Such strategies would be particularly important in a series based on the third pilot, that had relied upon modeling rather than overt lessons to make its point. What such strategies should be was left unspecified.

The research results also held something of a surprise, especially for the educators: the comprehension of children who discussed the shows with their teachers differed very little from the comprehension of those who did not. It seemed the use of the discussion topics in the teacher's guide and other printed materials did little to enhance the comprehension of the messages. The researchers noted that because the production of the pilots had been chronically behind schedule, the producer of the printed materials did not have adequate information about the content of the shows to use in developing these materials. The researchers concluded that better coordination between the television and print media components was necessary. The producer of the printed materials agreed strongly that more coordination was necessary, but also attempted, with some success, to discredit the research results that indicated that the printed materials added little to message comprehension. She argued that the teachers had not been instructed to use the materials in a manner that would have facilitated comprehension of the show's messages.

Whatever its limitations, the pilot research made important contributions to the development of the *Freestyle* strategy. The research gave the executive producer the go-ahead to use the dramatic third pilot as the prototype for the series, and it placed a major item on the agenda for design of the series — the development of a strategy to enhance message comprehension. The research, in fact, completed and made explicit the agenda for the entire *Freestyle* development process. This was the development of materials which were entertaining and understandable to children and acceptable to teachers. The third pilot was developed in the first place because the educators and researchers had argued that it could appeal to both teachers and children. The pilot research had explicitly tested and supported these arguments, but it had also shown comprehensibility to be important and problematic. The task ahead was, then, to design a series that capitalized on the educational acceptability and entertainment value of the dramatic format, but also improved its comprehensibility. The consortium's success in accomplishing this task is reviewed in Chapter 3.

DESIGNING THE SERIES

The pilot research, together with the judgment of the executive producer, had solved the problem of a general television strategy for *Freestyle*. The series would model activities, behaviors, and roles within a dramatic format. But this general solution created other, more specific, problems of its own. Indeed, designing the series was basically a working out of four problems created by the choice of the dramatic format and other constraints such as the curriculum plan and the young intended audience. One of these problems was, of course, enhancing the comprehensibility of the dramatized messages. There was also the problem of capitalizing on the educational acceptability of the dramatic format by planning coherent messages for each of the episodes. Similarly, a third problem was to develop printed materials which teachers could easily use to reinforce and expand upon those messages. Finally, there was the problem of capitalizing on the entertainment value of the dramatic format by creating characters and adventures that would appeal to children — especially boys who would probably be resistant to *Freestyle's* messages. In the course of solving these problems the executive producer and his advisers completed the *Freestyle* strategy.

The Problem of Message Planning

The executive producer and his advisers confronted the problem of message planning first. The educators had presented the executive producer with six subgoals and eighty-four objectives, and yet they also insisted that each of the eleven new episodes present only a few well-organized messages! Obviously the executive producer had to find a practical scheme for selecting and organizing content. In his search for such a scheme he rediscovered three themes proposed by the developmental psychologist: behavioral skills, nontraditional interests and activities, and adult work and family roles. He also rediscovered her idea of combining these themes within each show. In particular, he saw that the nontraditional interests and activities could provide the setting for, or springboard into, the events of each episode. The plot of the episode could then focus on the development or use of some behavioral skill. The executive producer characterized this as a "figure/ground" relationship and once he had consciously formulated it, he found it was already embodied in the third pilot. In that show the heroine's interest in auto mechanics had served as the springboard into the events of the plot. The plot itself turned on the taking of risks — both reasonable and unreasonable — by the girl, and on the nurturance of the male mechanic. The third pilot thus provided not only a general idea of the dramatic format, but also concrete model of the figure/ground relationship.

Using the three content themes and the figure/ground relationship as a scheme to plan the content of the shows, he tentatively laid out the eleven episodes. Based on the recommendation of the educators, about half of the shows would focus on girls. Most of these would have a behavioral skill as the figure with some pre-occupational activity as the ground. One or more of these shows could, however, focus on some particularly appealing nontraditional activity for girls as the figure itself. A smaller number of shows (perhaps three) would focus on boys, again with a behavioral skill as the figure and a pre-occupational activity as the ground. The other shows would focus on the adult work and family role theme. This tenative content plan was, in fact, closely followed in scripting the series. The executive producer thus had effectively and usefully reorganized the curriculum plan into his own system for thinking about the content of the series. This system not only reintroduced the three content themes as the basic structure of *Freestyle's* content, but it also established the relationship among these themes as the basic structure of the dramatic events to occur in most of the series' episodes. The system was, in turn, adopted as the basic structure of the summative evaluation measurement package (see Chapter 4). The revised curriculum plan was not forgotten, but the three content themes, not the goals and objectives, came to define the content of the entire series, the dramatic structure of each episode, and the outcomes for which *Freestyle* was eventually held responsible.

The Problem of Print

The problem of coordinating the printed materials with the television series came into sharper focus, at least for the executive producer, when he began to experiment with the content themes and the figure/ground dramatic structure in individual episodes. In one experiment, the executive producer chose independence as the figure and science as the ground. He quickly spun the web of a story around these elements in which a Hispanic boy and an Anglo girl must face intense peer pressure when they give up soccer and cheerleading to participate in the science fair. But when the executive producer began to outline the details of the story he encountered a problem. A story could not readily portray an abstract concept such as "science" and would have to model a concrete example of scientific activity. Television demanded that the concept be sacrificed to the example.

The work on this premise reminded the executive producer that television could not do everything and, at about the same time, the researcher's recommendation of closer coordination between the printed materials and television series reminded him that the printed materials could have a specific role. They could not only enhance comprehension of the messages more effectively than they had for the pilots, but they could also elaborate upon those messages. They could, for instance, provide more examples of scientific and athletic activities and help children to generalize from the concrete examples to the abstract concepts. They could also suggest the rich variety of relationships between pre-occupational activities and adult occupations. While the role of printed materials in conjunction with television had often been discussed by the consortium, these ideas had never before been formulated so clearly.

Both conceptual and scheduling problems remained in the coordination of print with television, but the printed materials for the series were much more closely linked to the messages of the shows than the materials for the pilots had been. The teacher's guide provided a number of discussion topics that would help children comprehend the messages of each episode, as well as activities that would help them apply those messages to their own lives. The guide also provided ideas that would help teachers infuse the *Freestyle* messages and materials into other curriculum areas. Thus, the printed materials came to play an important role in the *Freestyle* strategy and, as the summative evaluation would later show, made an important contribution to the success of the series. The teacher's guide, and indeed all of the materials, were well received by teachers even though the infusion strategy was less than successful. Teachers reported that they did not so much infuse *Freestyle* into their ongoing instructional program as force it into the program (see Chapter 3). More importantly, however, the summative evaluation showed the benefits of the series, unlike the pilots, were dramatically enhanced by the use of the printed materials in the classroom. The impact of the series on those children who both viewed the series and engaged in classroom activities outlined in the printed materials was substantially greater than on children who merely viewed the series (see

Chapter 6). The printed materials thus helped to accomplish the task of producing educationally acceptable materials and also helped to achieve the ultimate goal of changing children.

The Problem of Comprehensibility

Next, the executive producer confronted the problem of lower comprehension of the messages in the dramatic format. Even before the researchers had released their conclusions suggesting that this would be a problem, the executive producer spoke from time to time about the greater difficulty of developing messages about such abstractions as leadership and assertiveness compared to messages about the more concrete childhood activities. His own conclusion had been that the behavioral skills would simply require more screen time. The researchers had argued in their report on the pilot research, however, that merely increasing the screen time devoted to difficult objectives would not solve the problem:

> Explicitness in the portrayal of an objective rather than the length of a segment or the production technique seems to be the determining factor in the degree to which comprehension is achieved. . . . If a dramatic context similar to pilot III, which the children and teachers preferred, is to be used for the final series, then strategies must be undertaken to make the objectives more explicit.

The researchers did not specify any strategies, however.

One such strategy was, of course, to provide teachers with instructions in the printed materials for making the messages explicit. Another strategy, as proposed by the executive producer, was to include in each show one or more scenes in which the modeled behavioral skill was labeled and its components discussed by the characters. The same approach could also be used to relate pre-occupational activities to adult careers and to discuss changing adult roles. These scenes were to be worked into the plot and dialogue as naturally and realistically as possible. The executive producer called them "Ah-ha!" scenes because he hoped that upon seeing them children would exclaim "Ah-ha! Now I understand." The Ah-ha! scenes could also be supplemented in the school-use version of the series with a brief summary of the messages at the end of each show. The executive producer called these "classroom codas."

The reaction to the executive producer's proposal was mixed. The researchers supported the idea of making the messages more explicit by verbalizing them. Others argued, however, that the Ah-ha! scenes and the classroom codas would probably be bad television. If the messages were conveyed primarily through such scenes they would be dramatically isolated and easily ignored. Instead the messages should be so central to the story that the story itself, not a single talky scene, made the point. The executive producer responded that he and his writers would do their best to make the messages central to the stories, but that some strategy for making the messages as explicit as possible was still necessary. His defense of the Ah-ha! scene idea was bluntly practical: In the classroom, where the series would be the most thoroughly evaluated, children would be a captive audience and unable to escape talky scenes. The Ah-ha! scenes and classroom codas became part of the *Freestyle* strategy.

As it turned out, however, children viewing in class did manage to escape. The summative evaluation later revealed that while most children could recall many scenes of individual episodes, the Ah-ha! scenes were not often among them. However, the Ah-ha! scenes did tend to enhance message comprehension for children who could recall them. The summative evaluation also seemed to suggest that the best understood episodes are those in which messages are the most closely related to the story (see Chapter 3).

The Problem of Appeal

Finally, the executive producer confronted the problem of creating a living world of people and events to embody the dramatic strategy he had worked out to this point. The people and events of this world would, of course, have to effectively portray nontraditional activities, behavioral skills, and adult roles; but they would also have to appeal to children. Everyone in the consortium wanted a series that would appeal to all children, but they realized that would be difficult. The researchers pointed out that some earlier attempts to counter sex-role stereotypes had actually promoted resistance to nontraditional sex-role behavior among boys (see Guttentag and Bray, 1976; and Kob, 1975). The researchers also found that participation in nontraditional activities and behaviors varied greatly among both boys and girls. They suggested that those boys and girls whose activities and behavior were still quite traditional would probably be quite resistant to the series' appeal.

Based on these considerations the executive producer concluded that the characters and their adventures must have a special appeal to boys and to the "fence sitters" among both sexes. His strategy for appealing to these children would be to create characters who were themselves fence sitters — boys and girls who already had some nontraditinal interests, but who could still develop and grow in this regard. The male characters could become more nurturant and cooperative, but would remain masculine and would never ever be sissies. The female characters could become more independent, assertive, and effective leaders, but not at the expense of boys. Girls would be colleagues more than competitors and everyone would share in the rewards of nontraditional pursuits. There would, of course, be trials and tribulations along the way to these rewards, but the rewards would always come in happy — television style — conclusions to the adventure.

Freestyle would present a better world, but not a perfect one — there is no drama in perfection. In this world the inhabitants would be bigger than life, but not incredibly so — children would dismiss the incredible — and the virtue of nontraditional choices would always be rewarded. *Freestyle* would, then, portray a consistent and compelling world all of its own and this, as we shall argue in Chapter 5, is the key to its success. By vividly portraying a nontraditional world that works to everyone's benefit, *Freestyle* successfully promoted a number of more positive attitudes toward those who choose nontraditional pursuits and more positive perceptions of the competence of boys and girls, men and women in such pursuits. Significantly, it was often the boys who benefited the most from exposure to this world.

The World of *Freestyle*

The executive producer revealed the world of *Freestyle* to the consortium in the pages of the "writers' bible." According to the bible, the series would stress "the drama of the ordinary (that queasy, uncertain first day on the job; the awful fear of taking a chance in a nontraditional activity; that super feeling when you've tackled a new job and got it right)." The characters living out these dramas of the ordinary included six children and their families:

- Penny would be a 13-year-old, keenly interested in all things mechanical though also a little shy. Her widowed mother would run the family hardware store.

- Denice would also be 13, a natural leader and a fine athlete. Her mother would be an Asian-American and work as a bank loan officer. Her father would be an Irishman named "Red."

- Tess would be 11 years old and a traditional little lady. Her family would be the most traditional in the series.

- Marcus would be a black 13-year-old and the center of this circle of kids. He would be particularly popular because of his ability to organize the group's activities. His parents would run their own business together.

- Ramon would be a Hispanic 13-year-old who would often hide his nontraditional interests behind his athletic abilities. His father would run his own business and his mother would be studying accounting in conjunction with her bookeeping job.

⚹ Walter, Tess's older brother, would also be 13 and a budding
artist.

Following his master plan for the world of *Freestyle,* the
executive producer, assisted by a script writer, created these
characters to be active, interesting, and already somewhat
counterstereotypical — just the sort of kids with which the
fence sitters could identify. Particular care was taken to make
each boy attractive and competent yet "one of the guys."
Beyond these strategic concerns the executive producer concluded from his experience with the multiracial review board
that any characters exhibiting negative attributes must be
Anglo. Thus, it was Tess and Walter's family who was to be
most "traditional," though this family too was slated to eventually see the value of expanded roles for everyone. The minority
children and their families, on the other hand, were designed to
counter one stereotype or another. For example, Denice —
part Asian-American at the suggestion of an Asian-American
member of the review board — would be a fine athlete, somewhat emotional, and not always the perfect student.

These characters did not always develop on the screen
exactly as specified in the bible. In the case of Tess, the actress
cast did not lend herself very well to the role of a traditional
little lady and the character became a good deal more nontraditional early in the series. In other cases the limited number of
shows in the series and problems with particular scripts did not
allow all of the facets of each character to be developed. Interpretation of the bible was thus subject to the changing needs
of the series. The bible did, however, introduce all of the
featured characters, as well as record all of the major com-
mandments for writing the scripts. These included strict adher-
ence to the content themes specified as the figure and ground of
each episode, the inclusion of the Ah-ha! scenes, and the
development of a cliffhanger in the middle of the story to allow
it to be divided into two 15-minute chapters. The bible thus

summarized for the script writers those elements of the *Free-style* dramatic strategy that would impact most directly upon their work.

With the writing of the bible, the series design was complete. The executive producer had reorganized the content of the curriculum plan into a scheme he found useful for his own work and, in consultation with his advisers, laid out the plan for distributing the content among the shows. He devised the figure/ground and the Ah-ha! scene devices; he established the standard plot line of trial-and-reward; and, of course, he created the characters and setting of the series.

The advisers participated in this creative achievement by defining the problems and reinforcing the constraints within which the creative solutions had to be found. The educators, through the revised curriculum plan, defined the general contours of the series content. The researchers defined the problems of comprehensibility, coordination of the printed materials and the television series, and clarified some of the difficulties of appealing to children. The review board placed constraints on the design of individual characters. These problems and constraints, as much as their solutions, are responsible for the nature of things in the world of *Freestyle*.

PRODUCING THE SERIES

At last, a year and a half after the project began, production of the television series and the other materials could begin. As the executive producer geared up for this final task, he warned his advisers that earlier plans for extensive review and testing of the series scripts and shows were unrealistic, given the time available to complete them. The advisers demanded, however, that they be allowed to play some role in the production of the series, and after much discussion the executive producer and his advisers devised a production process that allowed the educators and researchers to retain their advisory roles.

The Production Process

One component of the production process was the premise team, composed of the executive producer, a second member of the television production staff, a curriculum planner, and a formative researcher. Its purpose was to carefully develop premises for the shows and thereby reduce, if not eliminate, the need for extensive review and testing of the scripts. The team was, however, to have some opportunity to review the scripts as they were written. Each member was responsible for collecting and introducing into the team's deliberations any data, critiques, or other relevant information to which they had access.

A second component of the production process was the curriculum assignment sheet (CAS). These sheets were, in fact, lengthy forms to be filled out by the premise team for each of the episodes. They were to serve as the agenda for the premise team's work and as the instructions to the writers of the scripts that would be developed from the premise ideas. Each CAS began with a brief summary of the episode's plot line to provide the writers with an overview of the show's content in the terms they would most appreciate—the story to be told. This was followed by a detailed presentation of the "figure" to provide a firm grasp of the primary educational message to be communicated. The next section was a detailed presentation of the episode's events ("plot points") in which the message was to be embodied. Later sections of the CAS detailed the Ah-ha! scenes and the relationship of plot events to specific outcome objectives. An appendix providing details of the "ground" (for example, a science fair experiment) concluded the document.

In overview, the premise team and curriculum assignment sheets were attemps to devise a workable premise generation and script development routine given the realities of the project. The premise team offered an opportunity for the educators and researchers to have some impact on the premises and scripts. Yet it also suited the needs expressed by the executive producer for a more streamlined advisory process. The CAS both structured the work of the premise team and enhanced communication between the advisers and the script writers. The elaborately structured instructions in the CAS were especially important because the script writers were to be working on a freelance basis and their only exposure to the content and design of the series, in addition to their relatively brief meetings with the executive producer, was through the CAS.

Premises

The premise team deliberated upon story ideas and prepared a CAS for each of the eleven new episodes. Some of the story ideas were developed by simply choosing a figure and ground from the content themes and then structuring a story to fit. Other story ideas, however, developed more spontaneously. For example, one premise began, according to the executive producer, with the image in his own mind of youngsters engaged in a home repair business. Penny, the mechanically inclined girl, was the natural choice for the lead and she was joined by Marcus, the young entrepreneur. These characters and setting then conjured up the image of feuding corporate executives and this image, in turn, suggested a plot. Penny and Marcus would begin a home repair business and work well together for a time. However, they would have an argument and split up. Attempting to work separately, they would soon learn that cooperation is best. Thus emerged a premise in which cooperation was the figure and mechanical interests for girls was the ground.

In generating premises, all of the members of the premise team suggested story ideas, though it was the executive producer who came up with most of the ideas which were actually used. But even when story ideas were not used they often sparked other useful ideas. The curriculum planner, for example, suggested a story idea involving the elderly. The story idea was not used, but it introduced onto the team's deliberations an activity — volunteer work in a senior citzens' center — which was later used as the ground for an episode about nurturant behavior by boys.

After the basic story idea emerged it was worked out in greater detail by the premise team and this was the point at which the objectives finally entered into the premise development process by suggesting directions for plot development. For example, a premise dealing with adult occupations and family roles focused on the experiences of Tess and Walter's mother reentering the job market. Once Mom has landed her job she could no longer be the family's full-time housekeeper so she develops a system for sharing the housework among the whole family. This plot point developed out of objective 2.8 in the revised curriculum plan:

> Children will recognize that in families where both partners work it is necessary for household responsibilities and child care to be shared.

Walter and Tess participate in Mom's plan, but Dad refuses to do so until the unfairness of his position becomes clear, even to him. This developed out of objective 2.9:

> Children will indicate that it is fair for adult males to assume a share of household responsibilities and child care.

Finally Dad pitches in and the whole family is happier. And this developed out of objective 2.10:

> Children will recognize that it is rewarding for all family members when fathers share in family responsibilities including caring for children.

The executive producer likened the use of the objectives in the development of the plot to a pilot's use of a preflight checklist. The relevant objectives reminded the team of the specific topics which should be included in a premise covering a particular content area. Another team member offered a different image of the process, however. He said that in at least some cases the plot became a garbage can into which as many objectives as possible were dumped. In any case, the specific outcome objectives were as much of a constraint on the development of the stories as a source of inspiration for them.

As the details of each story emerged the executive producer set to work preparing the curriculum assignment sheet to be used by the script writers. Early attempts to involve the whole team in actually filling out the CAS form led the executive producer to conclude that he alone should do the task. Even working alone a single CAS form took him about twenty hours to complete. The entire premise team did, however, review and critique the completed curriculum assignment sheets. The team's review sessions often included spirited debates, but the executive producer was always the final arbiter of disagreements. He used the team's comments to revise the CAS as he saw fit before passing it on to the writer to begin scripting.

The development of the premises for the series was, then, the point in which the educators and researchers on the premise team participated more directly in the actual creation of television than at any other time in the project. Together with executive producer they worked through the messages and story of each of the eleven new episodes. (See the Appendix A for a list of the messages and premise of each episode.) Still, it was the executive producer who generated most of the story ideas and who laid out the plot points. And it was the executive producer who in filling out the CAS translated the educational messages into the language of the writers.

Scripting and Production

As the executive producer completed each CAS he turned it over to one of the writers or writing teams he had recruited from the Hollywood talent pool. These writers were, for the most part, seasoned professionals with commercial television credits from such series as *The Waltons, Little House on the Prairie,* and *The ABC After School Specials.* The fact that these writers had prospered in commercial television suggests that they are well able to cope with severe constraints upon their work. Even so, these writers found the constraints imposed by the CAS and the *Freestyle* strategy in general more than they were accustomed to. Nearly all of the writers agreed that the CAS provided much more material than they needed. The plot points and a brief overview of the goals would have been adequate. But nearly all of the writers went beyond merely criticizing the CAS to enumerate the difficulties of attempting to include elaborate messages in a television show which is also to be entertaining.

Many of the writers saw a conflict between what the executive producer wanted and what they considered to be good television. "What I want is a story that is entertaining and amusing," said one writer. "What he wants is a story that teaches." This writer argued that the heavy emphasis on explicit representation of the message was a mistake because kids are sharper than they were being given credit for by the project. This writer was, however, not really unhappy with the script he had written because, like most of the other writers, he thought that he had found an acceptable compromise between presentation of the message and his own sense of good writing. He said that he achieved this by following his usual procedure of concentrating upon the characters. "I had to find the people I was going to write about. Explore them. Discover what they were like . . . what qualities they possessed in order to make the events of the plot real."

Another of the writers reacted still more strongly to the constraints imposed by the CAS and the series itself. He found the CAS to be confining, pedantic, and negative in tone. This writer concluded, like his colleague, that the series' approach underestimated the audience. He said that he would have preferred the approach of a network series for which he had recently written in which entertainment value was of first priority, but opportunities were still present to "make a statement." "That show was positive in values," he said, "but the producers were content with allowing the values to be inferred rather than hitting the audience over the head with them." As with all of the other writers who expressed some difficulty with their assignments, a recurrent theme in this writer's comments was the distinction between the affective and entertainment goals of most drama assignments and the cognitive and instructional goals of this assignment. The writers tended to view these as conflicting goals and often spoke in terms of finding some sort of compromise between them.

On the other hand, the writer who was the most positive about her assignment said that there was no real conflict between "educational needs and pure creative zest," though an important part of the script writing task was to bring them together. She also recognized a distinction between entertainment and educational goals, but spoke in terms suggesting synthesis rather than compromise.

In sum, the writers' responses to the curriculum assignment sheets and the *Freestyle* strategy in general display much variation. Taken together, they also highlight once again the problems of synthesizing entertainment and education within the form of television drama. But whatever the problems, these writers did all manage to complete a script.

The premise team reviewed all first-draft teleplays as the writers completed them. While the team's discussions ranged over a variety of issues, several major themes emerged. The curriculum planner served as the monitor of the realism of the scripts particularly in regard to life in the modern classroom. She enjoyed a good deal of success in convincing the executive producer and the writers that teachers do more that lecture to passive children. The formative researcher was primarily concerned with nonstereotypical portrayals, particularly of minorities. In addition to merely guarding against subtle racial/ethnic and sex-role stereotypes, he was always on the lookout for opportunities to involve the characters in a counterstereotypical behavior or situation. Both the curriculum planner and the formative researcher maintained pressure on the executive producer to include as much information, as possible in each show. Thus, for script development as for the previous tasks, the advisers on the premise team served to formulate the constraints within which *Freestyle* was to be created.

The premise team's critiques and suggestions were funneled back to the writers by the executive producer and incorporated by the writers into their drafts. The entire premise team reviewed a few of the second drafts, but often it was only the executive producer or the series' story editor. In all cases the story editor and/or the executive producer wrote the third and all subsequent drafts until the director took over to put the "director's polish" on the script. These last changes were often the sixth or seventh draft and were almost never seen by the premise team.

Premises were generated, scripts were written, and shows were produced simultaneously over a period of several months. Completed shows, according to the consortium's original proposal, were to be tested in a laboratory setting. Specifically, the proposal called for the shows in the series to be produced in clusters with a short period for testing between the clusters. The results were to be used to improve the shows in the next cluster. However, the shows were not produced in clusters, although the first two shows were tested. This testing indicated that children's interest flagged during talky scenes including the Ah-ha! scenes. The researchers concluded that a greater effort should be made in later shows to get the messages across in scenes with realistic action, particularly action involving children. This conclusion coincided with the executive producer's own judgment and the Ah-ha! scenes were "gentled" in the story editor's rewrites of the later scripts. The executive producer accurately characterized the later shows as relying on pure modeling and less on verbal mediation techniques such as labeling to present the messages.

While the shows were in production the other components of the consortium continued with their assigned tasks. Educational agency personnel prepared the materials for training teachers in use of the series and supporting printed materials. The community college prepared its outreach activities and the producer of the printed materials and her staff prepared the guides for the series. Even though the production of the series ran behind schedule, all of the materials were completed within ten months, in time for the scheduled premiere of the series on the Public Broadcasting Service. *Freestyle* went on to win a number of awards which recognized it as a significant creative achievement in children's television. These included awards from Action for Children's Television and The National Conference of Christians and Jews as well as an Emmy for a particular episode. In addition, as we will show in later chapters, *Freestyle* achieved many of its educational objectives as well. Though the series was rerun a number of times, the thirteen shows in this first season were also the last. The funder had provided funds for only a single season and no one was found to pay for any more.

CONCLUSION: *FREESTYLE* AS ORGANIZATIONAL PROCESS

Fundamental goals and concepts are not easily or directly developed into concrete educational messages and media materials. In the case of *Freestyle,* simple phrases such as "curriculum planning" and "series design" belie the complexity of the real development process. Curriculum planning, for example, must be understood in terms of organizational power and politics. Because power to shape the original curriculum was widely shared within the consortium, but agreement about its form and content was not, negotiation and compromise were necessary to the process. The development of the first curriculum plan, in particular, was marked by some tough politicking. The delineation of the problems with the first plan was a more skilled, but no less serious, exercise in organizational politics.

Once the general form and content of the plan had been bargained out and codified, other processes could operate. First, a single subject matter expert could be commissioned to outline the content. If any one individual can be credited with creating the curriculum, it was the developmental psychologist whose work provides the substance of the *Freestyle* curriculum. Then, the subgoals and objectives could be generated in a structured and orderly routine. The subgoals and objectives were, in essence, processed from the raw materials of the original curriculum plan and the developmental psychologist's document.

These organizational processes are quite clearly reflected in the products which they generated. The original curriculum plan was a vague and unsynthesized collection of ideas reflecting the many review and revision cycles in which it was pieced together. The retention of the key ideas from the original plan reflected the process of building a concensus on the need for a major revision of the plan. The real substance of the revised plan — "the specifics" — reflected the coherent ideas of a single individual — the developmental psychologist. And the list of goals and objectives in the revised plan reflected a routine which did little to synthesize or organize them into a strategy for changing the interests and attitudes of children.

These organizational processes were, then, adequate to collect a rich assortment of content ideas for the television series, but they were not sufficient to develop a strategy for effectively communicating that content. The curriculum plan remained to the end merely a list of goals and objectives very loosely organized by content. From time to time suggestions were made concerning strategy, but the consortium was never able to capitalize on them. In one instance the researchers suggested that the cognitive objectives should spell out the sort of information which could lead children to change their attitudes or expand their interests. For example, some early research had found that children justified their resistance to women holding many blue collar jobs with the argument that women do not have the necessary strength. This attitude could, the researchers argued, be attacked with the portrayal of such jobs as requiring skill rather than strength. This sort of strategic analysis of communication tasks was not systematically conducted, however. Knowledge and attitudes remained merely categories of objectives rather than elements of a strategy. Such strategic issues as organization of content into television messages was left to be worked out in the design of the pilots and the series.

The *Freestyle* strategy evolved in the process of designing the television shows which embodied that strategy. However, the strategy was not deduced from scholarly literature nor engineered from theory and research. Rather, it emerged in the solutions to creative problems — the problems of designing educational television that is readily comprehensible and well suited to classroom use yet also entertaining.

These problems were faced for the first time by the executive producer and his advisers in the development of formats for the three pilots. The short segment format of the first two pilots was chosen by the executive producer because he thought it would entertain children yet meet the condition imposed by the educators that the shows be divisible into two 15-minute segments. The dramatic format of the third pilot was a compromise between the executive producer's concern for entertainment value and his advisers' concern for educational acceptability. As it turned out, it was the third pilot which testing showed to be the clear choice of both students and their teachers. It was, however, the least understood of the three. It would be overdramatic to claim that in choosing the third pilot as the prototype for the series, the executive producer and his advisers chose entertainment over education. But it is clear that this choice reflected a deep concern for solving the problem of making educational television highly entertaining.

With this most basic strategic choice behind them, the executive producer and his advisers sought to synthesize entertainment value with comprehensibility and educational acceptability all within the form of television drama. First, the producer organized the messages into three content themes and then invented a dramatic structure for the messages (the figure/ground relationship). Then, in response to the problem of comprehensibility, he devised a mechanism by which the dramatized messages could be made more explicit and presumably more comprehensible (the Ah-ha! scene). Finally, the producer and his staff sought to embody these strategic elements in a television series which children — boys in particular — would not only want to watch, but also find convincing. The characters were human and likable, yet a little more attractive and a little more competent than in real life. Their adventures were set close to all children's lives and experiences — at home, in school, and in the community — yet were a little more exciting and much more satisfactorily concluded than real life. The characters and their adventures were a little bigger than real life. But then *Freestyle* was not supposed to be real life; it was supposed to be real television. Exactly how the *Freestyle* strategy would affect its audience — change attitudes and expand interests — was never explicitly formulated by the project staff. As we will argue in later chapters, however, the strategy does embody some current theorizing about how television can and does affect its audience. The project staff was not unfamiliar with these theories, but the strategy and materials were not developed from such theories; rather, they were developed through a process of problem formulation and solution. The advisers worked to define and clarify three basic creative problems — educational acceptability, comprehensibility, and appeal — and the executive producer worked to solve them. In the next chapter we will examine the success of the series in solving the three problems it was really designed to solve.

NOTE

1. The view of organizational politics developed here is most heavily indebted to the following work: G. T. Allison, *Essence of Decision* (Boston: Little, Brown, 1971); D. J. Hickson, C. R. Hinings, C. A. Lee, and R. E. Schneck, "A strategic contingencies theory of intraorganizational power," *Administrative Science Quarterly,* 16: 216-229. 1971.

Chapter 3

REACHING THE AUDIENCE

The *Freestyle* strategy and materials represent an attempt to solve three basic creative problems of educational television: producing a series which is acceptable to teachers, entertaining for its audience, and readily comprehensible to that audience. Solutions to these creative problems were clearly seen by the *Freestyle* developers to be necessary for achievement of their educational goal. A series acceptable to educators is, of course, necessary to gain wide use in schools. A highly entertaining series is vital in winning and holding viewers at home; and a readily comprehensible series is necessary to obtain the desired effects. In short, the television series must reach and then speak clearly to its intended audience. The search for specific strategies to solve these creative problems was reviewed in the previous chapter. The success of these strategies is the topic of this chapter.

ACCEPTABILITY FOR TEACHERS

The *Freestyle* developers' concern for educational acceptability imposed several constraints on the design of the series. The developers knew that *Freestyle* would have to compete for precious class time, and they were concerned that some educators would view entertainment and education as antithetical. One constraint was, then, that the series should be entertaining enough to engage children's attention, but contain coherent and overtly educational lessons. *Freestyle* absolutely could not appear frivolous. The developers also anticipated teachers' desire for quarter-hour segments so as to keep class time devoted to televised material within acceptable limits. At the same time, the developers were committed to half-hour episodes for home viewing. Thus, another constraint was that the series must consist of half-hour episodes each divisible into two quarter-hour segments. The half-hour home version and the quarter-hour school version could then be scheduled for appropriate time periods in the broadcast week.

Given these constraints, half-hour dramas promised to be a successful format for the series. Drama could engage 9- to 12-year-olds according to preliminary research yet could also facilitate the development of coherent lessons organized around an in-depth treatment of the topics. The divisibility constraint caused some problems for the creative staff until the executive producer hit upon the use of a cliffhanger scene at the midpoint of each episode. The half-hour drama could then be separated into two quarter-hour chapters. Further research showed a dramatic pilot with these characteristics to be the favorite of both students and teachers from among three different pilots. Drama became a cornerstone of the *Freestyle* strategy.

The lessons portrayed in the *Freestyle* dramas were summarized and presented to teachers in a guide to the series which included pre-viewing activities, post-viewing discussion topics and follow-up activities and exercises. The follow-up ideas included suggestions for "infusing" the lessons and materials into other curricular areas such as language arts and social studies if teachers could not devote time to career awareness per se.

In general, the strategy for making *Freestyle* particularly attractive and useful to teachers was to fit the television series and other materials as neatly as possible into the routines of teaching. In general the strategy was successful. Teachers who used *Freestyle* as part of the summative evaluation were enthusiastic. Among the 142 teachers in seven cities who used all the programs, 71 percent said that they would recommend *Free-style* "strongly" or "very strongly" to other teachers in their district. Another 24 percent said that they would recommend it with "some reservations." Only 4 percent said that they would have "serious reservations" and just 1 percent said that they would not recommend it at all.

A teacher from Kansas City described her response to *Freestyle* this way:

> The entire Freestyle program was terrific from the Freestyle Guide to the programs themselves. The content and presentation of the various segments were of such high quality. There were no "duds." There were no programs that did not stimulate discussion among the children. They literally begged to see it. Some of my "hardest to motivate" students asked when we were going to see Freestyle and would participate in the discussions and activities. I can't say enough good things. It has brought my children closer together as a group. They care more about each other. This is an added bonus. Freestyle — we'll miss you.

Such responses from the teachers who would recommend the series without reservation often focused on one or more of three themes. One such theme was the ability of the *Freestyle* dramas to engage the attention of students:

> Freestyle was entertaining while getting across its message. That was a prime reason for its success.

> The children were highly motivated to watch 'Freestyle.' In fact, if a child was absent he/she would take *it upon themselves* to watch the missed session at home or with another class.

> The shows certainly held the interest of the children. During viewing time, even though there were three classes (75 pupils) viewing at the same time you could hear a pin drop. The children loved the programs and were very attentive.

TABLE 3.1   Teachers "Grade" the *Freestyle* Shows

	Average Grade	Percentage			
		A	B	C	D-E
How well do the shows convey messages in a way that . . .					
(1) Holds attention of children?	A−	76	19	5	0
(2) Is clear?	A−	68	27	5	0
(3) Stimulates class discussion?	B+	47	43	10	0
(4) Is believable?	B+	48	42	10	0
Average of four grades	A−				

These comments coincide with the high "grade" teachers gave the series for its ability to hold children's attention (see Table 3.1).

A second theme in the comments of the teachers was the quality of experience which *Freestyle* provided to children beyond merely holding their attention. Many teachers noted that the series was more than a passive viewing experience. It was an active personal and social experience:

> It made learning fun and motivated many creative writing and art projects for us. It was such a good springboard for class discussions and we looked forward to each new show.

> I found it a series that was well acted, with believable situations, [actors] my children could identify with, interesting format and good subject areas.

> Children do seem to relate to these characters a few years older than themselves. They surely do find the situations believable, for after each show they're eager to share their own similar experiences.

These comments complement the high marks for the series' clarity of presentation and only slightly lower marks for its ability to stimulate class discussion (Table 3.1, rows 2 and 3).

Some teachers did find that *Freestyle's* insistence on always rewarding nontraditional behavior with a happy ending led to contrived plots at times:

> After awhile my class was able to predict the endings. The girl always saved the day. They were frankly getting tired of it.
>
> Some of the situations were very realistic — others were a bit too good to be true.

Still, the teachers easily passed the series on its believability (Table 3.1, row 4) perhaps because they realized that their own sense of believability was not that of their students. One teacher, for example, noted:

> Although children related well to the kids on the telecast I had trouble feeling they were believable. They were too good. I did hear this comment, but it may have been a reflection of my attitude.

The third theme in the comments of teachers focused on changes among the students:

> I think my students are much more aware of stereotyping and its results. Many changed their way of thinking or at least became more aware of stereotyping.
>
> Some of the things stressed in the shows stimulated a lot of their thinking and exploring the possibility of doing things on their own and showing more independence.
>
> During the bilingual episode, my *very* shy bilingual students blossomed. When I wrote all the possible careers they could go into on the board, and especially said, "Just think, Irene, these are all *your* possibilities when you grow up" — I've never seen this child look so pleased and proud. It was really touching.

In short, teachers liked *Freestyle* because they felt it worked.

The comments of the minority of teachers who had reservations about *Freestyle* also revealed three themes. Some teachers criticized the content of the series although their comments did not fall into any discernable patterns. The idiosyncratic nature of these comments suggest more that it is impossible to please everyone than that the series had specific problems with its content. The other teachers who had reservations commented not so much on the series itself as upon the fit of the series into their school. Some teachers complained that it imposed an overload on the already packed upper elementary curriculum. Other teachers reported inadequate access to television sets or other television-related problems (for example, poor signal reception) which made them doubt that the series could be easily used by other teachers, at least in their school.

Overall these comments and "grades" indicate that the strategy of using televised dramas to present the *Freestyle* messages to students was very acceptable to teachers. The teachers did indeed find *Freestyle* to be educationally worthwhile, but not simply because they thought it to be effective. Teachers were enthusiastic about the series specifically because it *combined* education and entertainment. The developer's concern that teachers would view entertainment and education as antithetical was, then, unfounded at least for these teachers and this series. At the same time, the comments and "grades" indicate that educational acceptability depends not only on teachers' perceptions of the quality of the materials, but also on the realities of life in the classroom. Insufficient time and inadequate television hardware are two such hard realities.

The relative success of the *Freestyle* strategy in gaining educational acceptance, as well as the nagging problems of insufficient time and inadequate television hardware, were also clear in teachers' evaluation of the two-chapter structure of each episode. Two-thirds of the teachers said that they would prefer to stick with the quarter-hour version rather than switch to the half-hour version for use in their classroom. The large majority accorded to the quarter-hour version vindicated the insistence of the educators among the *Freestyle* developers that this element of the strategy was important.

Even so, a third of the teachers said that they would have preferred to use the half-hour version in class. They gave two reasons. Some teachers cited adverse viewing conditions to support this preference. For example, one teacher who was adamant in her preference for the half-hour version explained that to view the series her class had to walk through three buildings to a cafeteria where they watched a single monitor along with three other classes. Under these circumstances the half-hour version shown only once a week simply would be less trouble. Other teachers cited lack of time to support their preference for the half-hour version. They argued that this version could reduce the *total* class time devoted to *Freestyle* even though it would increase the time devoted to the series on viewing days.

Of course, no strategies were available to the *Freestyle* developers to help individual teachers with the problem of inadequate hardware beyond making the half-hour version of the series available. Strategies were, however, available to help with the problem of insufficient time. Specifically, the strategy of "infusing" *Freestyle's* messages and materials into other curricular areas was intended to help ameliorate this problem. For example, a language arts assignment could be an essay on an episode of the series, while a math assignment could be the preparation of graphs showing the number of men and women in various occupations. *Freestyle* could thus serve as the content for instruction in the basic skills. Time spent on *Freestyle* could also count as time spent on reading, writing, and arithmetic.

In principle, the strategy was simple and elegant. In practice it turned out to be problematic. The teachers were asked if they had to "steal time" from other curricular areas to fit *Freestyle* into their schedule. In response, 36 percent of the teachers indicated that they stole "some time" and another 20 percent said they stole "a lot of time." For many teachers, then, *Freestyle* crowded out rather than infused into other curricular areas. *Freestyle's* particular infusion plans can, then, be credited with only limited success in overcoming the problem of insufficient time. It may be, however, that content and skill are intimately related in the minds of teachers and that any plans for infusing new content into existing skills instruction will have limited success.

In summary, *Freestyle* was well received by teachers though it did not — and probably could not — solve all of the problems confronting its educational acceptability. More than a quarter of the teachers participating in the evaluation reported that were it not for the special research situation they simply could not have spent as much time on *Freestyle* as they did. Competition for a place in the crowded school day will always be severe. Further, acceptance of materials that include television will continue to be hampered by inadequate hardware. Teachers participating in the *Freestyle* evaluation were in districts which had reasonably good television reception capability, but across the nation, 28 percent of the elementary teachers have no capability at all according to a survey by the Corporation for Public Broadcasting (Dirr and Pedone, 1979). Among those schools with reception capability the average ratio of classrooms to television sets is five to one.

These data suggest that the problems of insufficient time and inadequate hardware are insoluble for only a minority of teachers. However, these data along with CPB's finding that 57 percent of the nation's elementary teachers have not regularly used any of the many instructional television series now available provide a reminder that merely producing a series which teachers like and find useful does not guarantee wide acceptance. Still, the first step in gaining acceptance is producing such a series and *Freestyle* has demonstrated some useful strategies for taking this step.

ENTERTAINMENT VALUE FOR CHILDREN

Though *Freestyle's* entertainment value proved to be critical to its acceptance by teachers for classroom use, the developers' attention to entertainment had been motivated more by concern for home use than school use. The executive producer, in particular, had been a champion of the idea that the series must be highly entertaining so as to win and hold a home audience against the competition of other programs. He had come to favor the dramatic format when his judgment as well as research results indicated that drama could entertain 9- to 12-year-olds.

With the choice of format made, the executive producer and his staff sought to create characters and stories which all children would find entertaining and meaningful. The characters and their adventures were intended to be bigger than life, but not incredibly so. Strong female characters were, of course, central to the *Freestyle* message, but special care was taken to create attractive and competent male and minority characters as well. These characters would have a variety of adventures, but in the end they would all be rewarded for their nontraditional behavior. In general, the strategy was to package the *Freestyle* lessons in a slick Hollywood wrapping which children would easily recognize as entertainment.

Children's own evaluation of *Freestyle's* entertainment value coincided with that of their teachers. When children who had watched all the shows were asked how much they liked them both boys and girls were quite positive. On a 4-point scale ranging from "I like them a lot" (4) to "not at all" (1), the boys' average rating was 3.58 while girls' was 3.80 (Table 3.2, Q. 37). This difference is statistically significant given the large sample, but sex was not a powerful predictor of children's response to *Freestyle*. It accounted for only 2 percent of the variance in the ratings.

More informative is the children's comparison of the series to those they watch at home (Table 3.2, Q. 38). On a 4-point scale ranging from *Freestyle* was "a lot more fun" (4) to "a lot less fun" (1), the boys averaged 2.84 and the girls averaged 3.21. Girls liked the series more; sex accounted for 4 percent of the variance in the ratings. Thus against its competition at home, *Freestyle* fared somewhat better among girls than boys; but importantly, boys were not really very far behind.

These ratings come from in-school viewers in five cities, but in two other cities groups of children watched *Freestyle* at home. They were given a weekly reminder to view, but there was no pressure to view otherwise. Their viewing records shed more light on the attractiveness of the series for boys and girls. For any one of the *Freestyle* shows, 27 percent of the boys watched and 37 percent of the girls watched. Persistent viewing was also more popular among girls. While 12 percent of the girls watched seven or more shows, only 7 percent of the boys did.

Finally, the in-school audience that viewed in schools was asked to compare *Freestyle* to other school activities on the same scale used to compare it to other television shows. Not surprisingly, *Freestyle* fared very well against other school activities. The boys' rating was 3.55 and the girls' was 3.70. Here again the difference is statistically significant, but sex accounted for only 1 percent of the variance.

Black children rated the series the highest (3.78) and Mexican-Americans rated it the lowest (3.51), but race was not a powerful predictor of children's response either (see Table 3.2). It accounted for 1 percent of the variance in these ratings. Black children rated *Freestyle* highest against the home-viewing competition (3.21), while white children rated it the lowest (2.96). Minorities may have appreciated *Freestyle's* greater attention to minority interests compared to other programs. Still, the differences among the ethnic groups are very small. Race accounted for only 1 percent of the variance in the ratings. Similarly, in ratings against other school activities racial differences were quite small, with race accounting for less than 1 percent of the variance.

Overall, these data indicate that children found *Freestyle* to be an enjoyable experience. They liked the shows and, in fact, found them to compare favorably with other shows viewed at home. While boys rated the shows slightly lower than girls and were somewhat less likely to view, boys can hardly be said to be alienated by them. Children of varying ethnic backgrounds were also very similar in their enthusiasm for the shows.

TABLE 3.2   Children's Ratings of *Freestyle*

| QUESTION | AVERAGE RATINGS[a] | | | | | |
| | Sex | | Race | | | |
	Boys (2100)	Girls (2100)	White (3000)	Black (600)	Mexican-American (300)	Other Hispanic (100)
Q. 37: Overall enjoyment of *Freestyle*.	3.58	3.80	3.68	3.78	3.51	3.58
Q. 38: Comparison with TV series viewed at home.	2.84	3.21	2.96	3.21	3.11	3.18
Q. 39: Comparison with other school activities.	3.55	3.70	3.65	3.58	3.53	3.39

[a]Sample sizes are rounded to nearest 100; sex differences (*t* test) and race differences (*F* test) were all statistically significant at p < .001. Sex and race account for between 1 and 4 percent of the variance (eta-squared) in question responses.

Q. 37: "Overall, how much have you liked watching the *Freestyle* television show?" Responses were: "a lot" (4), "pretty much" (3), "a little" (2), and "not at all" (1).

Q. 38: "Compared to other shows you watch on TV at home, how much fun was it to watch *Freestyle*?" Responses were: "a lot more fun" (4), "a little more fun" (3), "a little less fun" (2), and "a lot less fun" (1).

Q. 39: "Compared to most other things you do in class at school, how much fun was it to watch the *Freestyle* television shows?" Responses were: "a lot more fun" (4), "a little more fun" (3), "a little less fun" (2), and "a lot less fun" (1).

The *Freestyle* strategy can be credited with success in providing an entertaining experience to boys and girls whatever their ethnic background. But just as the production of educational material that teachers like does not guarantee wide use, so the production of a television series that children enjoy does not guarantee a large audience. And just as systemic constraints outside of the control of the developers limit the use of *Freestyle* — or any instructional television series — by educators, so systemic constraints limit the home audience. In the case of *Freestyle,* the funder's failure to budget for promotion or for production of additional seasons of shows limited audience size. The Public Broadcasting Service's (PBS) scheduling of the series and the home audience's use of public television further shaped and constrained audience composition.

At the midpoint of *Freestyle's* three-month life on PBS it received a Nielsen rating of 2.2. This means that *Freestyle* was on in about 1.64 million homes for at least six minutes during the rating period. If this rating picture seems bleak it can be brightened a little by framing it within the ratings of other PBS children's series. Some examples: *Sesame Street,* 13.2; *Electric Company,* 7.6; *Zoom,* 3.4; *Feeling Free,* 0.9; *Infinity Factory,* 0.6; and *Villa Allegre* with an audience too small to measure. The higher ratings of such PBS hits such as *Sesame Street* and *Electric Company* may be due to higher intrinsic interest to their audience, but are certainly due also to such factors as promotion over a multiseason lifespan, more scheduled showings per ratings period, and broadcast by more PBS stations.[1]

Freestyle's ratings indicate that it reached 2.2 percent of the nation's television households, but more to the point is that it reached 5.5 percent of the households with 6- to 11-year-olds. Interestingly, it reached 9.3 percent of the households with children younger than six. This penetration of homes with children younger than the target audience was probably due in part to viewing by children in both age categories in the same household. In such cases the household would be counted in both categories. This penetration may also be due to the fact that many PBS stations scheduled *Freestyle* in the PBS "kiddie block" of programs in the afternoon and thus *Freestyle* received some of the "audience flow" from such programs as *Sesame Street*. The age of the audience for *Freestyle* thus reflected to some extent the age of the overall audience for PBS's children's offerings

Freestyle reflected the overall audience for PBS's children's offerings in other ways as well. Homes viewing the children's offerings are likely to have parents with above average educations. This was true of the homes viewing *Freestyle*. Homes viewing the children's offerings include disproportionately few minority families. This was also true of the homes viewing *Freestyle*. Homes viewing the children's offering are equally distributed in two income categories: $10,000-15,000 and more than $15,000. These homes are unlikely to have incomes less than $10,000, however. In this, *Freestyle* differed from the overall audience by attracting more households in the $10,000-15,000 category than in the more-than-$15,000 category.

In overview, *Freestyle* did not really fare badly in the ratings compared with other PBS offerings though it certainly could have done better. The summative evaluation data showed that the series had intrinsic interest for its intended audience, but other factors influenced audience size and composition as well. The size of the audience was limited by the show's short life, lack of promotion, and incomplete availability. The age of the audience was probably affected by the scheduling of the broadcasts. Other demographic characteristics of the audience were influenced by the pre-existing exposure patterns of various demographic groups. The potential of *Freestyle's* entertainment value, like its instructional value, thus was not fully realized. Still, *Freestyle* does provide an example of educational television which did have that potential.

MESSAGE CLARITY

Freestyle's dramatic format neatly solved the problem of combining educational acceptability and entertainment value.

With this format, lessons which teachers found worthwhile could be embedded in stories which 9- to 12-year-olds found interesting. In the dramatic pilot, for example, reasonable risk-taking had been instrumental to the adventures of a young girl in a nontraditional summer job. This format was not without problems, however. Research on the pilot had shown that children had trouble extracting the lessons from the stories. The strategy devised to deal with this problem was, first, to reduce the number of lessons in each story to no more than two closely related ideas (that is, the "figure" and "ground"). Next, these lessons were embedded in an interesting story just as in the pilot, but at some point in the story the lessons were verbalized by the characters in an Ah-ha! scene. In addition, a classroom coda which summed up the story and lesson was added to the end of each episode in the school version of the series. Of course, the school version was also to be used in conjunction with class discussions and activities led by the teacher.

The success of this strategy for making *Freestyle's* lessons explicit and comprehensible for 9- to 12-year-olds was assessed in extensive interviews with a sample of children in one of the summative evaluation sites. In this site, fourth and sixth graders from classrooms which had viewed and discussed *Freestyle* were interviewed after the series was completed. The children were asked a number of open-ended questions about each of several episodes including: "What do you think you could learn from that show?" These data are presented in Table 3.3. The answers to this question suggest that the comprehension strategies worked out by the *Freestyle* developers were not consistently successful. Most children could remember a lesson from the episodes, but these did not necessarily coincide with the lessons intended by the *Freestyle* developers.

An episode entitled "Hike" provides the most striking example. In this episode, Walter persuades his younger sister, Tess, to take a reasonable risk by going on a nature hike in search of rocks for her collection. On the hike, Tess lags behind the group and becomes temporarily lost. Later, when Ray takes

TABLE 3.3   Children's Report of Lessons Learned from Three *Freestyle* Episodes

Lesson Learned	Percentage of Children Reporting Lesson (N = 173)
(A) *"Hike"*	
Intended lesson: Risk-taking (e.g., "be willing to try new things even if you're afraid").	27
Secondary lesson: Sex role equality (e.g., "girls can climb mountains too").	7
Practical lessons: Nature hikes (e.g., "stay with the leader on a hike" "how to find fossils").	61
Other lessons	5
(B) *"Partners"*	
Intended lesson: Cooperation (e.g., "each one does part of the work").	40
Secondary lesson: Sex-role equality (e.g., "girls can fix things as good as boys").	30
Practical lessons: Business and finance (e.g., "how to earn money" "starting a business").	16
Social behavior lessons: Interpersonal conflict (e.g., "how to settle arguments").	10
Other lessons	4

(continued)

TABLE 3.3 continued

Lesson Learned	Percentage of Children Reporting Lesson (N = 173)
(C) "*Young and Old*" *Intended lesson:* Nurturance (e.g., "how to know about others feelings").	70
Practical lessons: The elderly (e.g., "old people aren't too different from young").	13
Social behavior lessons: Perseverence (e.g., "don't be a quitter").	9
Other lessons	8

an unreasonable risk and gets stuck on a ledge, it is Tess who facilitates his rescue.

This episode's primary lesson about risk-taking, so obvious in a plot synopsis, was much less obvious in the show itself according to the children. Only 26 percent of the children who said that they had learned something reported a lesson about risk-taking. Another 7 percent reported a lesson about equality of the sexes which is a secondary lesson of this and all other episodes. On the other hand, 62 percent reported a lesson about some more practical matter such as the importance of staying with the leader on a hike (Table 3.3A). The down-to-earth lessons learned by a majority of children, it must be recognized, were not wrong. Indeed, they were eminently reasonable lessons to have learned from this episode. They were, however, not the *intended* lessons.

A similar pattern of lessons emerged from an episode entitled "Partners." Here, however, a larger percentage of children did learn either the intended primary or secondary lesson. This episode featured Penny, who is skilled at household repairs, and Marcus, who is an excellent salesman. They agree to cooperate in a home repair business, but after working together for awhile they quarrel and split up. Soon they discover that they cannot make a go of it without the other's skill and they get back together. Among the children who said that they learned something, 40 percent reported a lesson about cooperation and 31 percent reported a lesson about equality. The others learned such practical lessons as how to begin a business or earn money or such social behavior lessons as how to deal with interpersonal conflict (Table 3.3B).

The most successful episode in getting across its primary intended lesson was "Young and Old." This is the episode in which Walter and Marcus volunteer at a senior citizens' center and begin to organize a sale of the seniors' crafts. Marcus is dismayed to find, however, that the seniors respond to his arbitrary and overtaxing schedule by walking out on the project. He and Walter then learn the importance of fully understanding the needs of others when trying to help them. The sale is a great success. Here 70 percent of the children reported a lesson about nurturance while most of the rest learned practical lessons about the nature of the elderly or social behavior lessons about preseverence (Table 3.3C).

Comprehension of the intended primary lesson thus ranged from about one-quarter of the children to about two-thirds. If children's overall comprehension of the intended lessons in these episodes is less than desirable, it is also instructive. The pattern of lessons learned from each episode and the variation in comprehension across episodes can serve as clues to help solve more effectively the creative problem of making lessons embedded in dramas readily comprehensible.

To summarize the clues: even after many weeks children could recall a reasonable lesson from these episodes. If children's comprehension is less than desirable it is not because they forgot or were confused about the right answers, but rather because many children were misled into accepting reasonable — though perhaps shallow — lessons about hiking safety, earning money, and the like. A solution to the problem of comprehensibility thus may lie in an explanation of how children could be led toward the intended lesson rather than misled toward the unintended lessons.

One explanation is that the dramatic organization of the shows themselves either helped or hindered comprehension of the intended lesson. In "Hike," the most poorly comprehended of the three episodes, the highly dramatic events of Tess becoming lost could certainly have led children toward the obvious, but unintended, hiking safety lesson and away from the more deeply embedded intended risk-taking lesson. On the other hand, in "Partners," which was somewhat better comprehended, the dramatic events surrounding the breakdown in cooperation could have been more helpful in leading children toward the intended lesson concerning the value of cooperation. And in "Young and Old," which was the best comprehended episode, the dramatic events of Marcus's insensitivity and the seniors' resulting walkout could have been very helpful in leading children toward the intended lesson concerning the importance of nurturing skills (specifically, empathy) in dealing with others. In short, the explanation is that those shows in which the drama is most intimately related to the intended lesson are the best comprehended.

Evidence for this explanation comes, first, from data on children's recall of the dramatic events of each episode and, second, from data on the relationship between recall of these events and the comprehension of the intended lesson. The children were asked as part of the interview to retell the story of each episode. Their responses were coded for recall of the six or seven key events or scenes of each episode. Table 3.4 presents the percentage of children recalling each of these scenes. Table 3.4 also presents the results of a Fischer's exact test on the relationship between recall of each scene and comprehension of the intended lesson. A low p-value indicates that a real relationship probably exists. Traditionally, in social science, a p value of .05 or less is required to say that a real relationship exists. Secondary lessons have been omitted from this analysis.

Table 3.4 holds few surprises in terms of which scenes were the best recalled. For "Hike" the scene of Tess becoming lost and panicking was by far the best recalled (Table 3.4A). "Partners" offers no scenes which were recalled as well as Tess's misfortune, but the scenes of Penny and Marcus's quarrel and splitup were the best recalled of the show (Table 3.4B). And from "Young and Old," Marcus's run-in with the seniors was the best recalled scene (Table 3.4C). These scenes are the cliffhangers. They are also precisely those scenes which — so the explanation goes — could lead children toward or away from the intended lessons. In contrast, the less dramatic and more talky Ah-ha! scenes which were explicitly designed to lead children toward the intended lesson were much less well recalled.

The real test of the idea that highly dramatic events in the story can lead children toward or away from the intended lesson is also found in Table 3.4. In "Hike" the dramatic and memorable scene in which Tess becomes lost is not associated with comprehension of the intended lesson. Thus, this scene does nothing to lead children toward the intended lesson. Neither does it do much to lead them away from it, however, though the nonsignificant relationship which does exist is negative (that is, recall of the scene is associated with learning an *unintended* lesson). This scene cannot, then, really be faulted with being truly misleading because children tend to recall it no matter what lesson they have learned.

If nearly everyone recalls this scene, then the recall of other scenes is likely to make the difference in lesson comprehension. Table 3.4A shows that recall of the Ah-ha! scene in which Walter persuades a reluctant Tess to take a reasonable risk and recall of the later scenes in which Tess's risk is vindicated by her rescue of Ray are all associated with comprehension of the

TABLE 3.4   Children's Recall of Scenes and Test of Relationship
Between Scene Recall and Message Comprehension in
Three Episodes of *Freestyle*

Scene	Recall (percentages)	Recall Related to Comprehension[a]
(A) *"Hike"*		
Tess is reluctant to go on a strenuous hike, but Walter convinces her its a risk worth taking because of her interest in nature (Ah-ha! scene).	36	.00
On the hike Tess lags behind the group to examine fossils.	50	.13*
Tess discovers she is lost and panics (cliffhanger scene).	86	.33*
Tess is found.	38	.49
Another member of the group, Ray, takes a dangerous short cut and becomes stuck on a ledge.	25	.00
Tess rescues him.	23	.00
(B) *"Partners"*		
Penny is skilled at repairs and Marcus is skilled at sales. They decide to cooperate in a home repair business (Ah-ha! scene).	27	.10
On their first call Marcus convinces a reluctant customer and Penny does a fine repair job.	11	.04*
They go on to do a variety of jobs together.	23	.14*
Their coordination of effort breaks down and they quarrel over who is boss (cliffhanger scene).	46	.35

TABLE 3.4 continued

Scene	Recall (percentages)	Recall Related to Comprehension[a]
They split up.	46	.01
Each tries to work alone but find that it is nearly impossible without the other's skills.	27	.01
They get back together.	30	.00
(C) *"Young and Old"* Marcus and Walter are assigned to report on a senior citizens' center as a project for school.	25	.17*
There they meet Rick, the center's occupational therapist, who interests them in volunteering.	4	.64
Marcus and Walter plan a sale of the seniors' crafts.	43	.08
Marcus gets carried away and prepares an arbitrary and overtaxing schedule for work for the seniors. They respond by walking out on the project (cliffhanger scene).	61	.01
Rick explains why the seniors quit. Marcus becomes upset and quits himself (Ah-ha! scene).	11	.05
Marcus's problem draws the attention of a previously uncommunicative senior who tells Marcus not to be a quitter. Marcus reconsiders.	35	.56
The sale is a success	29	.18

[a]Entries are the *p*-value of Fischer's Exact Test relating recall of this scene with comprehension of the intended message of the whole show.

*Negative relationship (i.e., recall of this scene is associated with comprehension of an *unintended* lesson rather than an intended lesson).

intended lesson concerning risk-taking. Thus it seems that when children come away from the viewing experience with a grasp of the events which propel Tess into her adventure and the happy conclusion, they are more likely to understand the intended lesson of that adventure. Unfortunately, only a minority of children come away with this complete a grasp of the story and therein lies an explanation of the poor comprehension of the intended lesson.

In "Partners" (Table 3.4B), the best-recalled scenes in which Penny and Marcus quarrel and then split up are markedly different in their relationship to lesson comprehension. The scene of the quarrel is not significantly related to comprehension of the intended lesson while the equally well recalled scene of the split up is related. Children who recall the quarrel itself are about as likely to learn the intended lesson as not, but children who recall the results of the quarrel — the split up — are more likely to learn the intended lesson. The finding that one of the best recalled scenes does little to lead children toward the intended lesson while the other one does, renders this episode's middling performance in lesson comprehension quite understandable.

In "Partners" as in "Hike" other less well recalled scenes were strongly associated with comprehension of the intended lesson. Children who recalled that after the split Penny and Marcus had a great deal of difficulty working alone and finally decide to cooperate again are more likely to learn the cooperation lesson. The relationship between the Ah-ha! scene and comprehension of the intended lesson is, however, not significant indicating, perhaps, that the discussion of cooperation in the scene was lost among the plans for starting the business and spending the earnings.

Finally, in "Young and Old" (Table 3.4C), the best recalled scene — Marcus's run-in with the seniors — is indeed related to comprehension of the nurturance lesson. The Ah-ha! scene in which Rick discusses nurturance is also related to comprehension of this lesson, but less strongly and very few children could recall the scene. The success of this episode thus rests squarely on its single most dramatic event.

Overall these results lend credence to the idea of an association between the dramatic organization of the story and the comprehension of the story's intended lesson. In "Hike," the vividly recalled drama did nothing to lead children toward the intended lesson and so they wandered off to reasonable, but unintended, lessons. In "Partners," the most dramatic events inconsistently lead toward the intended lesson and comprehension was only fair. In "Young and Old," the dramatic events did lead toward the intended lesson and this episode was the best comprehended.

This explanation of differences in comprehension across the episodes of *Freestyle* need not entail a simple causal relationship in which recall of particular scenes produces comprehension of particular messages though it is easy to slip into causal language when discussing the observed relationships. Rather, causality is likely to be mutual. That is, children simultaneously organize their grasp of the story and of the lesson into reasonable and coherent patterns of meaning. Similarly, they simultaneously retrieve from memory the story and the lesson. Each influences the other and together they form an overall pattern of meaning. These patterns vary across children and across episodes. Some shows readily lend themselves to patterns of meaning that include the intended lesson. Other shows do not. It is not enough to simply embed a lesson in an interesting story. And it is not enough to verbalize that lesson at some point in the story — such scenes may facilitate comprehension, but may not be very central to the drama and thus may not be well recalled. Rather, the drama must be so intimately related to intended lesson that they cannot be understood apart from each other. More than that, the drama must *be* the lesson.

NOTE

1. The series was aired by 185 of the 265 PBS stations when it premiered in October 1978. However, this rose to 230 by November 1978.

Chapter 4

EVALUATING THE EFFECTS

Freestyle was developed from four fundamental ideas. We have seen how the first idea — countering sex-role stereotypes — was developed into a highly detailed curriculum plan and how, in turn, this plan was used to help realize the second idea — production of a television series which was entertaining and comprehensible to children and acceptable to educators. We've also seen how the third idea — development of a process for creating such a series — was realized in the form of a consortium of organizations that labored more than two years to produce *Freestyle*. Now its time to see how the fourth idea was realized — evaluating the effectiveness of the whole enterprise.

To study *Freestyle's* effects, we at the Institute for Social Research undertook a field experiment which eventually included more than 7000 fourth to sixth graders in seven sites across the United States. Within these sites we divided the children into experimental groups ranging from intensive exposure to the *Freestyle* messages and materials on the one hand, to no exposure at all on the other. To each of these experimental groups we administered extensive questionnaires both before and after exposure. The details of the measures, the research design, and the data analysis are presented in this chapter. The ensuing chapters present some of the lessons we learned from our research.

THE MEASUREMENT OF *FREESTYLE'S* EFFECTS

Our work as summative evaluators, like the work of the executive producer and his advisers before us, was to have been guided by the goals and objectives specified in the curriculum plan. Like the executive producer and his advisers, we inherited a large and unwieldy plan which we attempted to simplify and reorganize. In doing so, we borrowed heavily from the executive producer's earlier attempt to reorganize the plan. The executive producer had identified three content themes — pre-occupational activities, behavioral skills, and adult work and family roles — which ran throughout the many goals and objectives of the curriculum document. He had used these themes as the basis for planning the content of the *Freestyle* series. Similarly, we used the themes as the basis for planning the measurement of *Freestyle's* effects. Within each of these general content themes the executive producer had selected from the curriculum plan specific activities (e.g., auto mechanics), skills (e.g., leadership) and adult roles (e.g., working mothers) to be featured in the series. These were the "figure" and "ground" for each of the episodes. Similarly, we used them as the content of questions to be asked of the children in our experiment. Thus, like the *Freestyle* series itself, the outcomes measured in the summative evaluation may be categorized into three content themes:

(1) *Childhood Pre-Occupational Activities.* These are activities which 9- to 12-year-olds often pursue and which may lead to specific career interests (nurturing activities for boys and mechanical, athletic, and scientific activities for girls).

(2) *Behavioral Skills.* These are skills which 9- to 12-year-olds can begin to develop and which are useful in careers (leadership, independence, assertiveness, and reasonable risk-taking for girls; helping skills for boys).

(3) *Adult Work and Family Roles.* These include frequently stereotyped adult activities both in the home (e.g., child care, cooking) and in the work place (e.g., specific occupations).

Beliefs, Attitudes, and Interests

In addition to these content themes, the outcomes that we chose to measure may be categorized in another way: by the type of effect upon the audience. One type of effect desired by *Freestyle's* funder and developers is increased interest in non-traditional pre-occupational activities and adult roles. In the long run, *Freestyle's* creators want children to be free of stereotypes in their choice of activities and roles. But in the short run they are willing to settle for expressions of increased interest in such activities and roles. Of course, interest in an activity or role does not ensure its later selection, but certainly lack of interest greatly hinders its selection. Increased interests are, then, a worthwhile — and measurable — potential effect of *Freestyle*. Accordingly, the effect of the series upon girls' interest in mechanical, athletic, and scientific activities, and boys' interest in nurturing activities along with both sexes' interest in nontraditional occupations, constitute the first category of effects measured in the evaluation.

Another category of effects was measured not because it was an explicitly stated goal of the funder or developers, but rather because we judged it to be a worthwhile and achievable effect of the series. Communication theorists have argued that exposure to the mass media shape the audience's perceptions or belief about what is true of the world. Social reality, they argue, is socially constructed and the media play a central role in the process.[1] An outcome of exposure to *Freestyle* may, then, be to change children's perceptions or beliefs about what is true of sex roles. For example, as a result of exposure to *Freestyle's* models of individuals who are successful in a variety of nontraditional pursuits, children may come to believe that more girls have leadership skills and mechanical ability than they originally thought. Similarly, they may come to believe that more adults occupy nontraditional work and family roles than they had previously imagined. *Freestyle* may, then, help to create a new sex-role reality for its audience.

The notion of altered beliefs about the world goes to the very heart of *Freestyle's* goals. The series seeks to counter stereotypes and in one sense of the term — perhaps the most important sense — stereotypes are a kind of belief. Specifically, stereotypes are oversimplified or distorted beliefs held by one group about another (see for example, Triandis, 1971: 103-112). For example, the belief that girls do not have mechanical ability or leadership skill is, by this definition, a stereotype. While altered beliefs are not explicitly mentioned among *Freestyle's* goals and objectives, any evaluation of a television series which seeks to counter stereotypes cannot ignore this effect. Altered beliefs, then, constitute the second category of effects measured in the evaluation.

To complete our list of effects we returned to the explicitly stated goals and objectives of the series. From the inception of *Freestyle,* its creators listed changed attitudes as a desired effect of the series. The curriculum plan is laced with references such as this one: "Children will affirm their acceptance of boys and girls performing nontraditional activities." Similar statements concerning the development of positive attitudes toward those who choose nontraditional occupations and toward girls who exercise independence, assertiveness, and leadership are found in the plan. Such attitudes are, perhaps, best labeled "norms" (Triandis, 1971: 115-117), and the desired effect of the series is, then, to shift children's norms regarding behavior appropriate to each sex. Changed attitudes or norms regarding the pursuit of nontraditional pre-occupational activities, behavioral skills, and adult work and family roles thus constitute the third category of effects measured in the evaluation.

These three categories of effects — increased interests, altered beliefs, and changed attitudes — together with the three content themes — pre-occupational activities, behavioral skills, and adult work and family roles — form the framework within which the outcomes of *Freestyle* may be organized. Table 4.1 visualizes this framework as a 9-celled matrix within which each of the specific outcomes is arrayed. This is the master measurement plan.

Developing Measures

Each of the specific outcomes in the matrix was measured with a multiple-question index. Five principles or rules were followed in generating these indices. The first was that they must be composed of closed-ended rather than open-ended items. This rule was necessitated by the plan to have teachers administer the questionnaire to their class as a group. Recording of individual answers to open-ended questions would not be possible. This plan was mandated by the economics of the large-scale, multiple-site research design. Based on these considerations, multiple-choice items were developed to measure each outcome.

The second principle was that a few simple question formats must be used. Most items followed one of a few basic prototypes. To measure attitudes the evaluative dimension used throughout was "very good idea" to "very bad idea." As an example, two of the items measuring attitude toward girls' participation in mechanical activities are given in part A of Figure 4.1.

For interests, the dimensions used were "like it a lot" to "don't like it at all" for pre-occupational activities and "definitely consider" to "definitely NOT consider" for adult occupations. In part B of Figure 4.1 are two items from the area of interest in pre-occupational activities. In part C are two items from the index of interest in adult occupations.

The measurement of beliefs required that a few beliefs be chosen for measurement from the enormous number which could conceivably be affected be *Freestyle*. We chose two beliefs which seemed particularly susceptible to change. One was the proportion of adults who occupy various roles (see part

TABLE 4.1 Typology of Dependent Measures

	Beliefs About	Attitudes Toward	Interest In
Childhood Preoccupational Activities	Boys in helping roles Girls in athletics Girls doing mechanics	Boys in helping roles Girls in athletics Girls doing mechanics	Helping Athletics Mechanics Science
Childhood Behavioral Skills	Girls as leaders Girls being independent Girls being assertive Girls taking risks	Girls as leaders Girls being independent Girls being assertive Girls taking risks	. . .
Adult Work and Family Roles	Sex of those in traditionally male jobs Sex of those in traditionally female jobs Wives doing male housework Husbands doing female housework	More women in "male" jobs More men in "female" jobs Wives doing more male household tasks Husbands doing more female household tasks	"Male" jobs "Female" jobs . . . . . .

NOTE: ". . ." indicates the concept was not measured.

D of Figure 4.1); the other was the proportion of children who are competent in various activities and skills (part E).

The third principle was that multiple items would be used to operationalize outcomes whenever possible. For example, the measurement of interest in mechanical activities included five items: (1) fix a broken bike, (2) build a model kit, (3) build a radio or something else that runs on electricity, (4) fix a leaky faucet, and (5) work with an adult on a car motor. Multiple-item indices, of course, help reduce measurement error and thus increase reliability compared to single-item measures. The indices were created from the individual items by first removing any items which were not consistent with the others and then computing the mean of the scores on the remaining items

The fourth principle was that each question must have a very concrete referent. For example, the index of interest in mechanical activities focuses on such concrete activities as "fixing bikes" rather than "repairing things." The indices are built up from a collection of concrete examples, because we assumed that children of this age — nine to twelve — think about their interests and attitudes at this very concrete level of abstraction.

The fifth principle was to include in each index some items which were explicitly illustrated in the *Freestyle* television shows and others which were not. The index for interest in mechanical activities, for example, includes two items explicitly covered in the shows (fix a leaky faucet and work with an adult on a car motor). The three other items were not explicitly portrayed. This procedure produces indices which can be subdivided to allow analyses either of the overall index or of the *Freestyle* subset, permitting a test of whether changes in the audience generalized beyond the very specific things viewed in the shows.

The 250 items developed from these principles were collected into a machine-scored questionnaire booklet entitled "My Interests Activities." Children completed these booklets both before the series premiered (September 1978) and again

A. Attitudes toward girls involvement in mechanical activities

How do you feel about GIRLS your age doing these things if they want to:

	Very good idea	Good idea	Bad idea	Very bad idea
fixing a broken bike	☐	☐	☐	☐
working with an adult on a car motor				
etc.				

B. Interest in pre-occupational activities

How much would you like to do each of these things if you had the chance?

	Like it a lot	Like it pretty much	Like it a little	Don't like it at all	Don't know what that is
fix a broken bike	☐	☐	☐	☐	☐
work with an adult on a car motor					
etc.					

C. Interest in adult occupations

It will be a long time before you choose an adult job. However, you probably know now that there are some jobs you would not consider doing and others that you would consider doing. What do you think about each of these jobs for yourself?

	Definitely consider	Probably consider	Probably NOT consider	Definitely NOT consider	I don't know what that job is
car mechanic	☐	☐	☐	☐	☐
truck driver					
etc.					

D. Beliefs about proportion of adults engaged in jobs

What do you think is true today? How many of the people who do each of these jobs are men and how many are women?

	Almost all are MEN	More than half are MEN	About half are MEN half are WOMEN	More than half are WOMEN	Almost all are WOMEN
car mechanic	☐	☐	☐	☐	☐
truck driver	☐	☐	☐	☐	☐
etc.					

E. Beliefs about proportion of children who are good at doing things

How many GIRLS are good at:

	All	Most	Some	A few	None
fixing a broken bike	☐	☐	☐	☐	☐
fixing a car motor	☐	☐	☐	☐	☐
etc.					

Figure 4.1: Illustrative Items from "My Interests and Activities" Questionnaire

121

after it concluded its first airing (January 1979). In one of the research sites, the children completed parts of the booklet a third time nine months later (November 1979). Each time the booklets were administered by teachers in four sittings that lasted from 20 to 40 minutes. The teachers read each question to the class in an effort to reduce the impact of reading ability on the responses. The teachers also filled out a "Student Characteristics Form" for their class which recorded sex, race, and other such information about each child. The analyses that follow are based largely on the data generated by these measurement instruments though occasionally the analysis draws upon children's responses to a number of open-ended questions which were asked by interviewers in one of the research sites.

In addition to these measures, all of which were designed to assess the effects of *Freestyle,* a number of other measures were also employed in the course of the research. After the series concluded the children rated the experience and compared it to school activities and television programs viewed at home. Teachers also rated the *Freestyle* messages and materials on a variety of dimensions. (These ratings by the children and their teachers, along with some of the children's responses to the open-ended questions, have already been reviewed in Chapter 3). Finally, the teachers kept detailed records of their use of the *Freestyle* materials.

THE RESEARCH DESIGN

Product Validation

The foremost question the summative evaluation was designed to answer is how well the *Freestyle* strategy works when it is used as its developers intended. In the natural settings of homes and schools there are, of course, barriers to such use. At school, teachers may not have enough time or equipment ot use *Freestyle* as intended and at home other television programs and activities compete for children's attention. To disentangle the effectiveness of the *Freestyle* strategy itself from the limitations imposed by such barriers to its intended use, we designed a field experiment in which *Freestyle* was used to best advantage. We call this approach to summative evaluation "product validation."[2]

Treatment Groups

The study included four experimental groups spread among the seven research sites. To assess the effects of *Freestyle* in the classroom, an experimental condition called "intensive school use" was created. In this condition the teachers in the participating classrooms were asked to do the following during each of the thirteen weeks which the series ran:

(1) Prepare the class for viewing the week's episode using the "Preview Activities" in the teacher's guide.

(2) Present the two quarter-hour segments of each episode on separate days.

(3) Lead a discussion after viewing each segment using "Talk Topics" in the teacher's guide.

(4) Conduct a supplementary activity suggested by the teacher's guide to reinforce the theme of the week's episode.

Clearly this weekly regimen demanded much of teachers whose school day was already crowded. Yet most of the teachers we asked to participate did spend the required two hours per week. Of the 141 teachers who were originally assigned to this condition, 116 were judged to be in full compliance with the requirements of the condition. This meant that they presented 25 of the 26 quarter-hour segments to their class, led preview and follow-up discussions for 24 of those segments, and conducted a supplementary activity in 11 of the 13 weeks. The classrooms of teachers who were not in full compliance were excluded from the data analysis.

To assess the effects of *Freestyle* when viewed at home, two experimental conditions were created — "school/view only" and "home view." The "home view" condition, like all of the other conditions, included complete classrooms of children to facilitate administration of the experiment, but in this condition the children viewed *Freestyle* at home. When the series premiered, the school sent letters to parents asking them to encourage their children to view the series. By random assignment some parents were also asked to view with their children and discuss the shows afterwards. On Fridays during the experiment, teachers reminded their students to view the show over the weekend and on Mondays they had their students indicate on a chart whether or not they had viewed.

We anticipated, of course, that exposure to *Freestyle* would be much lower for home viewers than for school viewers. Indeed, researchers attempting to assess the effects of *Sesame Street* and *Electric Company* had reported difficulty in getting children to view enough episodes to claim to have actually exposed them to the series. As it turned out, about 25 percent of the students in our home viewing condition viewed seven or more of the episodes in the series and each episode was, on the average, viewed by about one-third of the students. For public television this level is quite high, but for our purposes it was still very low.

To avoid some of the problems of earlier research we established another experimental condition called "school/view only" which was designed to supplement the home use condition. In this condition the teachers in participating classrooms provided an opportunity for their students to view each of the 26 quarter-hour segments. However, the teachers were asked not to discuss the series or conduct any related activities. To minimize the possibility of spontaneous class discussion, an effort was made to schedule the viewing just before recess. While this condition is not a perfect surrogate for home viewing, it does reflect the ability of the *Freestyle* series alone to affect children. Of the 41 teachers who were originally assigned to this condition, 29 exposed their classes to 25 of the 26 episodes and were thus judged to be in full compliance with the requirement of the condition. Data from these 29 classrooms are presented in Chapter 6.

The fourth condition in the experiment was the control condition. In this condition teachers in the participating classrooms did not expose their students to any of the *Freestyle* materials or messages.

Seven Research Sites

These four conditions were established in the seven research sites as shown in Figures 4.2 and 4.3. The schools in each site were matched on several demographic characteristics and then randomly assigned to one of the conditions established in that site. All of the participating classrooms within a school building were assigned to a single experimental condition. The intensive school use condition was established in five of the research sites. In three of these — Long Beach/Torrance, CA; Milwaukee, WI; and Ann Arbor, MI — the intensive school use of the series was compared to the control. In the other two sites — Worcester, MA and North Kansas City, MO — intensive school use was compared to both the control and school/view only. Finally, in Covina, CA and Saginaw, MI viewing occured at home. Home viewers were compared with controls.

Administrative considerations such as teacher training and television delivery requires that a "treatment" be clustered in a single geographical location such as a city. But statistical confidence is somewhat diminished when the target audience is chosen from only one site. To increase confidence in the findings, each treatment condition was established in at least two locations. By using identical procedures in both locations, the findings in one site could be verified in the other. Viewing-plus-discussion was considered the most important treatment since it would provide the benchmark for the amount of change

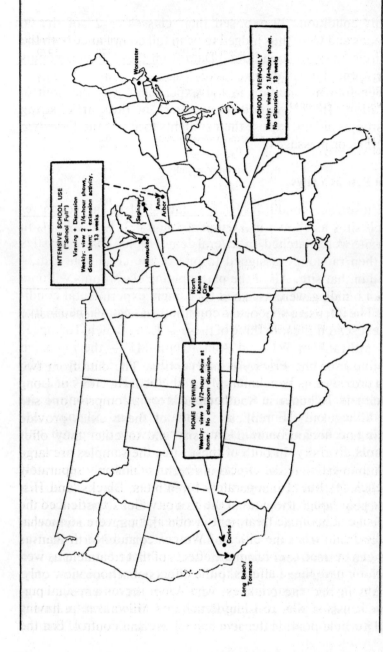

Figure 4.2 Test Sites for Evaluation of *Freestyle*

	September 1978	January 1979	November 1979
Site Type 1: Intensive School Use (Viewing plus discussion)	0_1 Classroom view + discuss $0_a \ldots 0_n$ 0_1 School Control	0_2 0_2	(0_3) (0_3)
Site Type 2: School/View only	0_1 Classroom view + discuss $0_a \ldots 0_n$ 0_1 Classroom view only $0_a \ldots 0_n$ 0_1 School Control	0_2 0_2 0_2	
Site Type 3: Home Viewing	0_1 Parent-Child view + discuss 0_1 Child/view only 0_1 Home Control	0_2 0_2 0_2	

Figure 4.3 Schematic of the Research Design

NOTE: Where 0_1 = pretest, 0_2 = posttest, 0_3 = post-posttest (0_3 in Ann Arbor only), and $0_a \ldots 0_n$ = intermediate measures.

possible from the *Freestyle* intervention. The data from two sites provide this benchmark: The neighboring cities of Long Beach and Torrance in Southern California comprise one site and Milwaukee the replicate. Both of these cities provide ethnic and socioeconomic diversity and together they offer regional diversity. In both of these sites the samples are large enough to estimate the effects of *Freestyle* not only separately for each sex but also separately for Whites, Blacks, and Hispanics. Although the sizes of the groups which experienced the intensive school use treatment in other cities were somewhat smaller, data from the cities of Worcester and North Kansas City can be used to confirm the effects of that treatment as well as to compare those effects to the effects of school/view only.

Among the research sites, Ann Arbor serves a special purpose. It was similar to Long Beach and Milwaukee in having just two treatments: intensive school use and control. But the students provided additional data unavailable in any of the other cities. At the beginning of the study they completed only part of the master paper-and-pencil questionnaire ("My Interests and Activities"); in return for this lightened load they provided face-to-face interview data. After the students had been exposed to the entire series each student again completed sections of the questionnaire and then participated in a half-hour interview which probed their views of nontraditional sex roles and then asked them to recount the story line and messages of a number of the shows. Finally, nine months later the Ann Arbor students completed the questionnaire for a third time, providing data on the persistence of effects.

In Table 4.2, the seven sites are listed along with the sample sizes used in the analyses. The numbers exclude students who were in "underimplementing" classrooms and students who did not provide data both before and after the experiment. Table 4.3 breaks down the students in the Long Beach site by their demographic characteristics. The data show that the various categories of sex, grade, and race are represented adequately to permit estimating each group's response. The split of boys and girls is approximately equal; grade four and grade six students each compose at least one-third of the sample permitting good representation of the two extremes in the age range of the target audience. Whites comprise 69 percent of the sample; Blacks and Mexican-Americans 16 and 15 percent respectively. The data from Milwaukee show a similar demographic distribution (demographics from other sites are in Appendix C).

DATA ANALYSIS

The remaining chapters examine the effects of *Freestyle* on beliefs, attitudes, and interests. In each chapter, two basic questions are addressed: What were children like before *Freestyle* and how different were they afterwards? The first question addresses the issue of the need for an intervention like *Freestyle;* the second the issue of effects.

TABLE 4.2   Sites and Sample Sizes

			SAMPLE SIZE FOR ANALYSES*		
SITE	TREATMENT	Group	Schools	Class-rooms	Students
Long Beach/	Intensive	View/Discuss	13	25	585
Torrance, CA	Classroom	Control	7	16	363
	Use	Total	20	41	948
Milwaukee, WI	Intensive	View/Discuss	13	36	784
	Classroom	Control	5	14	247
	Use	Total	18	50	1031
Ann Arbor, MI	Intensive	View/Discuss	7	16	477
	Classroom	Control	2	5	112
	Use	Total	9	21	589
Worcester, MA	Classroom	View/Discuss	5	23	421
	Intensive	View Only	5	15	375
	and	Control	3	12	268
	View Only	Total	13	50	1064
North Kansas	Classroom	View/Discuss	6	14	310
City, MO	Intensive	View Only	6	12	245
	and	Control	0	0	0
	View Only	Total	12	26	555
Saginaw, MI	Home	View	6	11	252
	Viewing	Control	2	4	99
		Total	8	15	351
Covina, CA	Home	View	6	11	315
	Viewing	Control	2	4	112
		Total	8	15	427

*Classroom sites: Students present at both testings and teacher implemented treatment at very high level. Home sites: Students present at both testings.

These questions can be elaborated with the help of Figure 4. 4. The first question (question A in Figure 4.4) asks what children were like before the intervention. This requires looking at their position on some scale, such as interest in mechanics. Implicit in a sex-role intervention such as *Freestyle* is the notion that boys and girls are different on the topics chosen for the series. For example, the intervention exists because it was thought that boys are interested in mechanical endeavors while girls are

TABLE 4.3   Characteristics of Long Beach Sample After Eliminating
            Low Implementing Classrooms (N = 948)

	n	percentage
Treatment		
Control	363	38
Experimental	585	62
Sex		
Girls	435	46
Boys	513	54
Grade		
Four	310	33
Five	237	25
Six	401	42
Race		
White	649	69
Black	155	16
Hispanic/Mexican origin	144	15

not, and *Freestyle* is needed to enhance girls' interests to make
them more like that of boys. The question of need, then, asks
where does each group lie on the scale. Are girls at the end of
the scale corresponding to "not interested in mechanics?"
Since scales are all relative, we would like to comment on
whether the girls' level of interest is appreciably different from
that of boys. In other words, how big is the gap between the two
groups? The statistic used in this book is *d*, the difference
between the average score for boys and girls divided by the
standard deviation of the measure.

Covariance and Statistical Significance

Question B asks whether *Freestyle* changed the experimental groups relative to the controls. Again there are two questions implied here. The first is whether at the time of the
posttest the difference between experimentals and controls is
statistically significant. Given that it is, the second question
follows: How big was the impact of *Freestyle* on the experi-

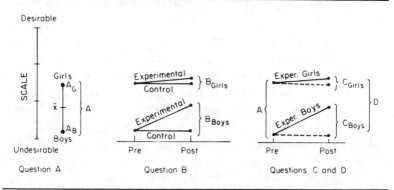

Figure 4.4 Patterns in the Data

Question A: What were boys and girls like before *Freestyle*?

Question B: Did *Freestyle* change the experimental groups by a statistically significant amount relative to the control groups?

Question C: If yes to B, by how much did the experimental groups change (educational significance)?

Question D: Was the gap between boys and girls perspectives reduced? (D vs. A)

mentals? Consider the issue of statistical significance first. In this study this is tested using analysis of covariance predicting the posttest score while covarying the pretest score. Analyses are done separately for boys and girls. The covariance strategy is used to adjust for pretest differences between experimentals and controls. The random assignment of schools to treatments was effective enough that experimental and controls were equivalent at pretest, and covariance was not strictly necessary; but the technique did serve to smooth out minor variations in pretest means for experimental and control students.

The unit of analysis is a controversial issue today. Cronbach (1976) has argued that the most appropriate unit of analysis in studies such as this is the school, since that is the unit at which the random assignment occurred. Our feeling is that *Freestyle*, while it was delivered similarly within each school, was processed differently by each individual within each classroom. We were not comfortable covering up that variation by aggregating to the classroom or school level. If the data were to be aggregated, the classroom would be the highest level, since there is considerable variation in effect size among classrooms in the same school, suggesting that teachers differed somewhat in how they presented material. Reflecting these considerations, the data in the next two chapters are presented using the student as the unit of analysis. However, parallel covariance analyses were done aggregating to the classroom level. In almost every case there was agreement; where there was not, the decision on effects was the more conservative one, with a nonsignificant difference indicated in the tables.

One other criterion for effectiveness was used. As explained earlier, multiple sites were chosen for each treatment. Thus intensive school use was implemented in both Long Beach and Milwaukee. To increase confidence in the findings, we required replication of the Long Beach findings in Milwaukee. Since intensive school use was a part of the treatment plan in Ann Arbor, Worcester, and North Kansas City, findings in these sites were also used when the findings in Long Beach and Milwaukee were in disagreement.

Educational Significance

To say that exposure to *Freestyle* leads to a statistically significant difference between experimentals and controls on some outcome dimension says nothing about the "educational significance" of the effect (question C in Figure 4.4). With samples of children as large as 1000, small differences between groups are very often statistically significant. Given that an experimental group is significantly "better" than a control group at the time of the posttest, the next question to ask is whether the difference is big enough to be educationally significant or important. Importance is very difficult to define when the measures being analyzed are scales with such relative anchors as "good idea" and "bad idea." Some yardstick is needed which indicates how big a difference is "big." Cohen (1977) advocates that the difference between the posttest means for the experimental and control groups be caluculated and divided by the pooled posttest standard deviation (SD). Using this method has the advantage of standardizing the measure of effects across different scales, and therefore different studies. These differences can then be compared to norms for small and large effects. At this point in time, norms for effect size are somewhat arbitrary. Cohen himself proposes that .20SD be judged as a small effect, .50SD a medium effect, and .80SD a very large effect. Horst and Tallmadge (1976), based on their experience evaluating educational programs, suggest that a difference of one-third of a standard deviation can be considered "educationally significant." Indeed, this norm is advocated in the *Ideabook* (Tallmadge, 1976) which is used to provide guidelines for the certification of new educational products by the Department of Health, Education, and Welfare Joint Dissemination Review Panel. Experience at the Institute for Social Research with two national studies of high school aged youth ("Youth in Transition" and "Monitoring the Future") suggests norms only slightly different from these. A difference of .20SD is the threshold of something interesting, .22SD-29SD a modest effect, .30SD-.39SD a sizable effect, and a shift in excess of .40SD a very large effect. These are the norms which are used in the present study.

A small modification of Cohen's formula increases its utility in this study. The usual approach is to compare the posttest means of the experimental and control groups and divide by the pooled posttest standard deviation. However, the relevant question is how much of a change in the experimental group came about as a result of exposure to *Freestyle*. This suggests taking the difference between the pre- and posttest scores for just the experimental group and dividing by the pooled pretest standard deviation. If there has been random assignment to the experimental and control groups, and if there indeed has been no significant pretest/posttest shift on the part of the control group, this procedure will yield essentially the same results as Cohen's approach since the control group's score on the pretest should be the same as the control group at the time of the posttest. In addition, using the pooled pretest standard deviation avoids the bias frequently introduced when the standard deviation for the experimental group shifts at the time of the posttest.

Using the pretest standard deviation permits making yet another comparison of interest in a study such as this which has differential goals for boys and girls (question D in Figure 4.4). One way that sex-role stereotypes manifest themselves is that on measures of sex role beliefs boys and girls are far apart; that is, there is a gap between their views. A goal of *Freestyle* is to reduce this gap, so it is necessary to be able to talk about the size of the gap at pretest and posttest in a comparable metric. For a given measure, one can take the difference between the group means for boys and girls at either pretest or posttest and divide this by the standard deviation of the pretest measure for the pooled sample of experimental boys and girls to come up with a measure of the gap which is standardized. This method permits comparing gaps at two points in time as well as shifts across time in a comparable metric — a metric for which some norms exist for what is small and large.

An example is provided in Figure 4.5. Attitudes toward girls in athletics is measured on a 4-point scale, ranging from one (it's a very bad idea) to four (it's a very good idea). At the time of the pretest the overall mean on this scale for all respondents is 2.75 with an SD of 0.94 units. The average for girls is 3.08 and boys 2.47. Are the two groups far apart initially? A calculation of the difference in SD units — $(3.08 - 2.47)/.94$ — indicates a difference of .64SD, or two-thirds of a standard deviation. This is a very large difference. Do the boys change as a result of their *Freestyle* experience? Their average movement is from 2.47 to 2.93, a shift of .48SD — again, a very large difference. The girls

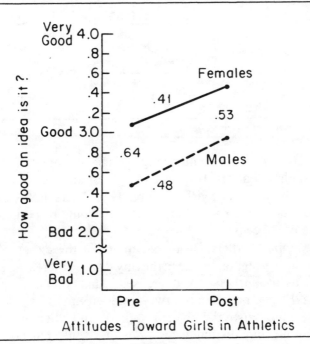

Figure 4.5   An Example Showing SD Shifts

also changed by a very large amount, .41SD. At the time of the posttest the gap between boys and girls' attitudes was reduced to .53SD.

There is one other complexity to keep in mind in judging the effects of *Freestyle*. The goals of *Freestyle* permit several different patterns of outcomes to be considered evidence of success. Three such patterns are shown in Figure 4.6. Pattern A shows the entire experimental group, both boys and girls, starting at an undesirable point on some scale and being moved by the *Freestyle* experience to a more desirable point on the scale. This is clearly evidence of success. For example, if both boys and girls believed that adult jobs such as mechanic or doctor were held only by men, then the hope would be that

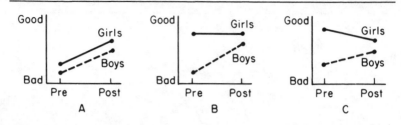

Figure 4.6 Patterns of Positive Effects

exposure to *Freestyle* would change this belief equally for both boys and girls. Pattern B is an example of an area where the target is only boys. The girls are already at the desirable end of the scale, and movement of just the boys would be considered evidence of success.

In example C there is no movement of the experimental group in the aggregate, because the boys' score increases about as much as the girls' score decreases. This is an example of reducing the gap between the two target groups. It would be a desirable effect when the object is beliefs, and when one group is holding an unrealistically high position, one that could be characterized as a defensive posture. Consider, for example, boys and girls estimating how many girls are capable of being good leaders. At the time of the pretest the girls think that all girls make good leaders and boys think no girls make good leaders. *Freestyle* might moderate the extreme views of both groups and in so doing, bring the perceptions of the two groups closer together. This could be judged a positive effect, because a shared view of reality will enhance girls' chances of achieving leadership positions. Another reason for judging such a pattern positively is that interventions of this type have the potential to polarize one of the target groups. Guttentag and Bray (1978) found that adolescent boys and girls became more polarized after their sex-role intervention. A similar experience occurred in Germany with preschool children. A special segment designed to reduce sex-role stereotypes was inserted into the German version of *Sesame Street*. After viewing these segments the boys were more sexist (Kob, 1975). Experiences such as these lead us to judge positively a series which does not polarize the sexes, and instead reduces the gap between boys and girls. This pattern, however, can be detected only by examining the pattern for experimental boys and girls. While it is not a common occurrence, we do find a few examples of it in the results for *Freestyle*.

NOTES

1. Perhaps the best known communication theorist in this regard is George Gerbner who along with his colleagues has argued that commercial television cultivates a view of the world as violent, dangerous, and just plain mean at least among heavy viewers (see, for example, Gerbner and Gross, 1976). While Gerbner's work has its critics (for example, Hirsch, 1980), the idea of socially constructed reality has a good deal of currency in communication research. Berger and Luckman (1966) provide a general introduction to the general idea.

2. Details of the "product validation" approach are provided in Johnston (1981).

Chapter 5

CHANGING THE AUDIENCE WITH
VIEWING AND DISCUSSION

The *Freestyle* strategy was developed primarily to produce
television which was comprehensible and entertaining for children and acceptable to educators. It did not arise out of theory
or research about how to bring about lasting effects on children.
The dramatic format, for example, had been chosen not because it was known to be an effective way to increase interests
or change attitudes, but because children liked it and teachers
found it acceptable for classroom use. Other elements of the
Freestyle strategy, such as the Ah-ha! scenes and the figure/
ground plot structure, were designed to increase the comprehensibility of the messages embedded in the dramas. Still,
we would argue that the strategy which finally emerged is a
coherent and promising approach to achieve the sort of effects
which we have chosen to measure: increased interests, altered
beliefs, and changed attitudes.

The *Freestyle* strategy for increasing children's interest in
nontraditional pursuits is to model those pursuits attractively.
When, for example, Ramon and Walter tutor a younger child in
English, they model not only a specific nurturing activity, but
also the pride of a teacher whose pupil has mastered a new skill.
Similarly, when Walter and Tess's mom takes a job outside the
home, she provides not only a model of a working woman, but
also someone who finds satisfaction in her work. Such images
planted in the minds of children may well blossom into the
increased interests which the *Freestyle* developers seek.

However, *Freestyle* is more than a collection of interesting
and rewarding pursuits displayed by attractive models. It is a

world all of its own. In the world of *Freestyle* everyone is willingly, even joyfully, breaking free of the old stereotypes. Marcus and Walter, for example, learn helping skills when they volunteer at a senior citizens' center, and Tess learns to take reasonable risks when she has the opportunity to go on a strenuous hike. Breaking free of stereotypes is not without difficulties, but ultimately it is always rewarding. Marcus and Walter, at first, misunderstand the needs and abilities of the senior citizens, but finally organize a highly successful project with them. Tess feels humiliated when she becomes lost, but sticks with it to become a hero when she rescues someone else. It's all quite natural for boys to be nurturers and girls to be risk takers in the world of *Freestyle*. And it is quite possible that exposure to this world can alter children's beliefs about the capabilities of boys and girls. *Freestyle* can, then, help to create a new sex-role reality for its young audience.

The world of *Freestyle* is not the real world of 9- to 12-year-olds, but neither is it beyond credibility. The inhabitants of this world are not beyond recognition and their adventures are not beyond imagining. But more than this, *Freestyle* is a *meaningful,* if different, world because it is internally consistent and true to its own nonstereotyped principles. In this world, nontraditional choices are encouraged and supported, though for the sake of a good story such choices are not always easy or unopposed. Chris must overcome Mat Morgan's reluctance to hire a girl as his helper in the service station and Walter and Tess's dad is not enthusiastic about his wife's job in a factory. Sooner or later, however, everyone comes to agree that nontraditional choices are not merely tolerable, but quite appropriate and very rewarding. In the world of *Freestyle,* changed norms about appropriate behavior yield richer and more satisfying lives. Exposure to this world may, then, not only alter children's beliefs about what is true of their own world, but also change their norms or attitudes about what is appropriate in their world.

In summary, the *Freestyle* strategy is to do what television does best — provide attractive models and, more than that, create a consistent and compelling alternative world. When used in the classroom, the strategy is also to do what teachers can do best — serve as personal guides to this world and help their students feel at home in it. Whether or not this strategy can really produce any of the measured effects when used to best advantage — intensive school use — is the topic of this chapter. First, we will consider the effects of *Freestyle* on children's interests, then the effects on beliefs and attitudes in each of the three content areas. Finally, we will review the degree to which these effects persist over a nine-month period.

INCREASING INTERESTS

We begin our search for effects with *Freestyle's* most difficult task: changing children's interest in activities considered nontraditional for their gender. Why children's expression of interests and not their actual behaviors? After all, the funders and designers wanted to change the way children behave. If only girls paid more attention to their own intrinsic interests, they argued, and less to society's expectations, many more girls would join football teams or help their dad fix the car. While changed behaviors — a girl actually joining a team or working on a car motor — is the ultimate goal, it seemed unreasonable to us to hold a television series accountable for this. Behavior is determined by many factors outside the sphere of television's influence, including opportunity (the availability of a team to join), skill, and social support. A less stringent criterion, but a barometer of future behavior, is a person's expression of interest in performing activities.

We begin this section by asking two questions. Before viewing, were children's interests in *Freestyle* activities sex-typed? The answer to this question helps us gauge the audience need. Second, does *Freestyle* alter this pattern, reducing the predictive power of gender?

Childhood Activities

Freestyle emphasized four nontraditional activities: nurturing activities for boys, and mechanics, science, and athletics for girls. The measures we developed to gauge interests consist of a question stem followed by a list of specific activities which fall into each of the interest categories. The stem is: "How much would you like to do each of these things if you had the chance?" There are five response possibilities: (1) "don't like it at all"; (2) "like it a little"; (3) "like it pretty much"; and (4) "like it a lot." An additional category allows for the alternative, "don't know what that is." The specific activities in each of the four interest categories are:

- *Interest in Mechanical Activities:* How much would you like to:
  - (1a) fix a broken bike
  - (1b) build a model kit
  - (1c) build a radio
  - (1d) fix a leaky faucet
  - (1e) work with an adult on a car motor
- *Interest in Scientific Activities:* How much would you like to:
  - (1n) raise goldfish at home
  - (1o) watch the stars and planets and figure out the names of groups of stars
  - (1p) make an insect collection (ants, moths, butterflies, or other insects)
  - (1q) make a collection of different kinds of rocks
  - (1r) read books about rocks, insects, flowers, or stars
  - (1s) do a project for a science fair
- *Interest in Athletics:* How much would you like to play:
  - (1u) football
  - (1v) basketball

- (1w) dodgeball
- (1x) soccer
- (1y) basketball
- *Interest in Helping Activities:* How much would you like to:
  - (1f) take care of a younger child at the playground
  - (1g) help a younger child with math
  - (1h) teach a younger child how to play a game
  - (1i) sew a button on clothes or sew up a tear
  - (1j) help an adult fix meals for the family
  - (1k) help old people (not living in your home)
  - (1l) help at a recreation center for handicapped people who are deaf, crippled, or blind
  - (1m) take care of sick people (not living in your home)
  - (1t) run errands for an elderly person

An "index" of interest in each of these categories was constructed by averaging responses to items in each category. Thus a respondent's "interest in mechanics" is defined as the average interest in doing each of five specific mechanical activities.

Initial Differences. The developers chose these particular activity categories because they thought boys and girls differed in their interest in them. In other words, they thought the activities were sex-typed. The data in Figure 5.1 reveal how well the developers chose the activities to be emphasized. Before exposure to *Freestyle,* girls did indeed show very little interest in mechanics. Their mean of 1.87 is below "like it a little." Boys, on the other hand, are at 2.85, close to "like it pretty much." This difference in standard deviation units is 1.23SD. As explained in Chapter 4, this is an extremely large difference, indicating that mechanical interests are indeed sex-typed and an appropriate target for *Freestyle.*

A related domain is interest in science, but it is not nearly as sex-typed. Girls average 2.71 and boys 2.95. In SD units this is

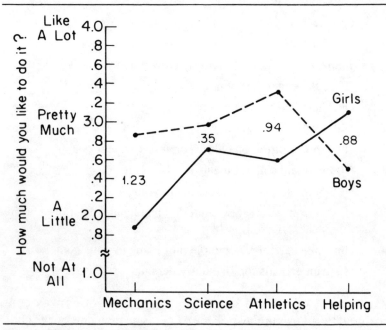

Figure 5.1   Interest in Childhood Activities: Pretest Differences for Boys and Girls
(Holland Job Classifications)

moderately large (.35SD); but note that girls are near the scale point, "like it pretty much." This same pattern was found in North Kansas City and Ann Arbor. In Worcester and Milwaukee, the boy-girl difference was even smaller. Boys and girls in Milwaukee were virtually identical at 2.92. Scientific interest may have been an unnecessary target for *Freestyle*. This argument rests on the definition of "scientific interest" in this study, and the reader is left to judge whether or not the items represent interest in investigative activities. The items were chosen with the aid of elementary and junior high science teachers who were asked to identify behaviors typical of 9- to 12-year-olds which they would judge to be indicators of scientific interest. The items do not include activities with a mechanical or technological component. The items are less "active," perhaps, than tearing down an engine or constructing a rocket. They include reading, observing, collecting, and classifying. It seems, however, that these activities are at the heart of what science is all about. Since the one "science show" in the series involves conditioning the behavior of goldfish for a science fair project, the items clearly reflect *Freestyle's* version of science.

Girls show a modest interest in athletics; the mean is 2.58, half-way between liking it "a little" and "pretty much." But boys are much more interested as indicated by the difference of .94SD units. Athetics appears to be an appropriate target for *Freestyle*.

Helping activities were included because they are assumed to be sex-typed as female. Indeed, this is the case. Boys show a modest interest in nurturing activities while girls "like it pretty much." The difference is .88SD — a very large difference.

In sum, three of the four targeted childhood activities in the *Freestyle* series are sex-typed and appropriate targets for an intervention.

Effects of Freestyle. Freestyle's impact on these interest patterns is shown in Table 5.1. Recall from chapter 4 that three criteria must be met to say that *Freestyle* was effective. (1) At the time of the posttest the difference between the experimental and control groups must be statistically significant. (2) The movement for the experimental group from pretest to posttest, measured in standard deviation units, must be "educationally significant," defined as at least .20SD units. (3) The findings must replicate in two sites.

Girls showed a moderately large shift in mechanical interests (.29SD), but the resultant interest level was only 2.10, corresponding to "like it a little." Girls' interest in science was unaffected, and boys' interest in helping activities was affected by a small amount, .22SD.

Freestyle altered girls' interest in athletics by a very large amount, .45SD. Before exposure, girls' interest was midway between liking it "a little" and "pretty much" (2.58); afterwards

TABLE 5.1 Interest in Childhood Activities

Interest in . . .	GIRLS			BOYS		
	Mean Pretest	Mean Posttest	SD Difference	Mean Pretest	Mean Posttest	SD Difference
1. Mechanical activities	1.87	2.10	.29	2.85	2.88	.04
2. Scientific activities	2.71	2.75	.06	2.95	2.93	(.03)
3. Athletic activities	2.58	2.93	.45	3.31	3.40	.12
4. Helping activities	3.09	3.19	(.15)	2.50	2.65	.22

NOTE: Data are for the experimental group only. If the "SD Difference" figure is in parentheses, the experimental/control comparison was not significant at $p < .05$. See Chapter 4.

it was quite close to "pretty much" (2.93). This shift is quite impressive; however, it did occur in only one site, Long Beach. Milwaukee and Worcester girls were much more interested in athletics to begin with. In Milwaukee, girls, interest increased from 2.93 before *Freestyle* to 3.07 afterwards. This increase of .19SD falls short of "educational significance." It is noteworthy, however, that the posttest interest scores in Milwaukee and Long Beach were very similar. Perhaps, if the target audience is "in need," as appeared to be the case in Long Beach, *Freestyle* can meet the need.

All in all, the *Freestyle* experience did alter some interests in nontraditional pre-occupational activities, but the pattern is inconsistent. Only girls' interest in athletics increased by a large amount.

The Specifics of Change. Each of the four indices used above is composed of a short list of activities. Some of the activities were explicitly illustrated in the programs; others were not. For example, "interest in mechanics" is composed of five activities. "Fixing a leaky faucet" was illustrated in the show "Partners," and "working with an adult on a car motor" was a central theme in "Grease Monkey." The other three mechanical activities were not illustrated in any of the shows. As explained in Chapter 4, measuring the concepts in this way permits examining whether change occurs only for show-specific activities or generalizes to the broader domain. For childhood activities the data do not provide a clear picture regarding generalization. For mechanical interest there was a much larger effect for just the *Freestyle* activities — .42SD for the index composed of just the two *Freestyle* activities and .29SD for the index composed of all five activities. For interest in athletics, the effect was about equal; the combination of soccer and football showed a shift of .42SD while the effect for all five sports was .45SD. For helping activities, the effects were larger with the non-*Freestyle* activities included — .22SD versus .10SD. Based on just these four indices the picture is unclear, but it appears that the effects are not limited to only those activities illustrated in the shows — the effects can generalize as well.

Adult Roles

The ultimate goal of *Freestyle* is to affect the orientations of children when they become adults. Do children's interest in adult jobs reflect a sex-typed orientation to the roles they will fill as adults? To find out, we asked them this question regarding their expectations when they become an adult.

(Q. 14) When you grow up, do you expect that you will have a job outside the home? [Yes, I definitely will; Yes I probably will; No, I probably will not; No, I definitely will not].

Their responses to this question are shown in Table 5.2. Before *Freestyle,* the average response of boys was 3.61, halfway between "definitely" and "probably" will have a job. Girls were one-half a standard deviation lower at 3.25; this is a large difference, but on the average girls are still above the "probably" point. A companion question asked about expectations for a spouse.

(Q. 15) If you get married, would you want the person you marry to have a job outside the home? [Yes, definitely; Yes, probably; No, probably not; No, definitely not].

Here the contrast between boys and girls is much sharper. Girls' expectations regarding a husband averages 3.46 — almost as high as the boys' own expectations of working. However, boys do not reciprocate. Their average response is 2.48, half-way between "probably" and "probably not." Certainly, not much can be read into these responses as indicators of future behavior. Further, we do not know to what extent either sex was considering children when they responded. However, the responses do suggest that boys may be the group most in

TABLE 5.2 Interest in Adult Jobs

	GIRLS			BOYS		
	Mean Pretest	Mean Posttest	SD Difference	Mean Pretest	Mean Posttest	SD Difference
(Q. 14) Job outside home?[a]	3.25	3.38	.18	3.61	3.63	(.04)
(Q. 15) Spouse have a job?[a]	3.46	3.54	(.07)	2.48	2.66	.17
Number of jobs "considered"[b]						
Total jobs (36 max.)	15.2	17.6	.28	15.3	17.3	.24
Male jobs (25 max.)	8.6	10.5	.29	12.3	13.6	(.19)
Female jobs (11 max.)	6.6	7.1	.15	3.0	3.8	(.23)
Percentage male jobs	56.4	59.6	(.12)	80.4	78.6	−.12
Percentage female jobs	43.6	41.4	(−.12)	19.6	21.4	.12

NOTE: Data are for the experimental group only. If the "SD Difference" figure is in parentheses, the experimental/control comparison was not significant at p < .05. See Chapter 4.

[a]Response scale: Definitely yes = 4, probably yes = 3, probably no = 2, definitely no = 1.

[b]"Considered" includes responses "probably," or "definitely would consider" when it's time to choose an adult job.

149

need of change if women are to participate more actively in the labor force, since boys are more resistant than girls to having a spouse work. As the data in Table 5.2 show, exposure to *Freestyle* raised girls' expectations about their own prospects for working and boys expectations for their spouse, but not quite by an amount considered in this study to be "educationally significant."

"What do you want to be when you grow up?" The fact that females anticipate working outside the home as adults is not the only — or even the best — indication that they expect to play nontraditional roles as women. The type of work they are interested in is also significant. To assess the career interests of both sexes we asked them:

(Q. 6) It will be a long time before you choose an adult job. However, you probably know now that there are some jobs you would not consider doing and others that you would consider doing. What do you think about each of these jobs for yourself? [Definitely not consider, probably not consider, probably consider, definitely consider].

The list of jobs presented to them was constructed to represent several different ways to divide up the world of work. These include sampling from Holland's six basic job types; sampling both "masculine" and "feminine" jobs; and representing *Freestyle*-emphasized jobs versus similar, but nonemphasized jobs. All of the 36 jobs on the list meet the criterion of being "familiar" to 9- to 12-year-olds, as determined by three consultants for the career development exercises of the National Assessment of Educational Progress. In some cases job "titles" were supplemented with descriptions to ease comprehension problems for this age group. The jobs are presented below with wording exactly as it appears in the questionnaire. (Jobs were not identified as "male" of "female.")

"MALE" JOBS

| *Car mechanic* | pharmacist (gives out medicine | owner of a business which makes |

truck driver

electrician

carpenter

worker in a factory
who puts things
together (like a car
or other machine)

machinist (makes
parts for machines)

boss in a factory

professional
athlete

coach

reporter
(writes stories
for a newspaper)

photographer
(takes pictures
for a newspaper)

in a drug store)

geologist
(scientist who
studies rocks)
and minerals

designer of
electrical things
like TVs, radios,
or calculators

scientist who
studies how the
weather works

scientist who
studies how
plants and
animals grow

designer of
airplanes
or rockets

*owner of
a hardware
store*

things like shoes,
toys, or furniture

manager of a
motel or hotel

owner of a
restaurant

owner of a
company which
builds houses

sales person
in a store
who sells cars
or televisions
or refrigerators

*city council
member*
(someone
elected to
run a city)

someone who
sorts mail in
the post office

"FEMALE" JOBS

Nurse

school teacher

librarian

dental assistant
(clean people's

*teacher of
children
who have
problems
with seeing
or hearing*

homemaker

secretary

bookkeeper
(keep records
of money spent
and received
by a business)

teeth or help	(a father or	check-out clerk
dentist fix)	mother who	at a grocery
their teeth)	stays home	or discount
	and cares for	store
occupational	the children	
therapist (help	cooks meals	telephone
sick or old people	and cleans	operator
learn new skills)	the house)	

Jobs in italics were portrayed in at least one *Freestyle* episode. This means that an appealing adult — frequently a parent or "significant other" of one of the teenage stars of the show — filled the role. Of the ten featured jobs, seven were portrayed by adults of the nontraditional gender; mechanic, coach, and teacher of the hearing impaired were not.

Male and Female Jobs. Let us begin an examination of effects on children's career interests by dividing the jobs into groups of traditionally male and female jobs. The data are easiest to appreciate if the response scale is first collapsed, such that responses of "definitely" and "probably would consider" are treated the same. If a child gave either of these responses to a particular job then we interpreted it to mean that he or she would "consider" this job. The data are displayed in part 2 of Table 5.2. Before *Freestyle,* girls and boys both "considered" the same number of jobs; about 15 jobs out of a possible 36. Differences arise when the lists of "considered" jobs are broken down by sex-type. Boys' lists were composed of 80 percent male jobs while the lists for girls had only 56 percent male jobs. Clearly, by the upper elementary years girls and boys show interest patterns which reflect the more traditional patterning seen in American society. Does exposure to *Freestyle* increase children's interest in nontraditional jobs? Girls and boys alike lengthened their list of "considered" jobs by two. But when the composition of the lists is examined, it turns out that the basic pattern is scarcely changed. Girls' lists are still comprised of less than 60 percent male jobs, and boys' lists about 80 percent male jobs. Overall, it appears that the intervention was not strong enough to alter the occupational interest pattern of children.

Holland Job Types. The 36 jobs can also be divided into six groups according to the Holland occupational scheme. John Holland, a vocational psychologist, has developed a theory of occupational choice that has relevance for a sex-role intervention such as *Freestyle* (Holland, 1966). He postulates that all people can be classified into one of six basic personality orientations or types. Associated with each of these types is a cluster of jobs to which people of that type gravitate. As a result, jobs can be characterized according to the predominant type of person filling the job. The relevance for this study is the fact that several of the six personality types, and hence job clusters, are characterized as "masculine" or "feminine." A brief description of each of the types and their associated occupations appears below. The exemplary occupations in the descriptions are those in the *Freestyle* list of 36 — a listing purposively contructed to sample each of these six types.

HOLLAND JOB CATEGORIES[1]

REALISTIC. The model type is masculine, physically strong, unsociable, aggressive; has good motor coordination and skill; lacks verbal and interpersonal skills; prefers concrete to abstract problems; conceives of himself as being aggressive and masculine and as having conventional political and economic values. Persons who choose or prefer the following occupations resemble this type: [examples used in the *Freestyle* research are] car mechanic, truck driver, electrician, carpenter, worker in a factory who puts things together (like a car or other machine), machinist (makes parts for machines).

INVESTIGATIVE. The model type is task-oriented, intraceptive, asocial; prefers to think through rather than act out problems; needs to understand; enjoys ambiguous work tasks; has unconventional values and attitudes; is anal as opposed to oral. Vocational preferences include: pharmacist, geologist, electrical engineer, meteorologist, biologist, aeronautical engineer.

SOCIAL. The model type is sociable, responsible, feminine, humanistic, religious; needs attention; has verbal and inter-personal skills; avoids intellectual problem solving, physical activity, and highly ordered activities; prefers to solve prob-lems through feelings and interpersonal manipulations of others; is orally dependent. Vocational preferences include nurse, professional athlete, coach, school teacher, librarian, dental assistant, occupational therapist, teacher of children who have problems with seeing or hearing, homemaker.

CONVENTIONAL. The model type prefers structured ver-bal and numerical activities and subordinate roles; is con-forming (extraceptive); avoids ambiguous situations and problems involving interpersonal relationships and physical skills; is effective at well-structured tasks; identifies with power; values material possessions and status. Vocational preferences include: secretary, postal clerk, bookkeeper, check-out clerk at a grocery or discount store, telephone operator.

ENTERPRISING. The model type has verbal skills for selling, dominating, leading; conceives of himself as a strong, masculine leader; avoids well-defined language or work situa-tions requiring long periods of intellectual effort; is extracep-tive; differs from the Conventional type in that he prefers ambiguous social tasks and has a greater concern with power, status, and leadership; is orally aggressive. Vocational pre-ferences include owner of a hardware store, owner of a busi-ness which makes things like shoes or toys or furniture, manager of a motel or hotel, owner of a restaurant, owner of a company which builds houses, sales person in a store who sells cars or televisions or refrigerators, city council member.

ARTISTIC. The model type is asocial; avoids problems that are highly structured or require gross physical skills; resem-bles the Intellectual type in being intraceptive and asocial; but differs from that type in that he has a need for individualistic expression, has less ego strength, is more feminine, and suffers more frequently from emotional disturbances; prefers dealing with environmental problems through self-expression in artistic media. Vocational preferences include newspaper reporter or photographer.

From the descriptions it is clear that the most "feminine" jobs are in the social and conventional categories, while the most "masculine" are in the Realistic and Enterprising categories.

The essence of Holland's theory concerns the way in which personality types and job types become linked. He posits that individuals seek out job environments where the predominant personality type matches their own personality type. To make this match individuals utilize stereotypes of people who work in different jobs. What more obvious stereotype is there than the sex of the people who usually hold these jobs? *Freestyle* must break down this stereotype if it is to successfully change the target audience. But it is clear from Holland's theory that more than gender is involved in the stereotype; it is the type of person as well, many of whom's characteristics may transcend gender.

Classifying children's interests by the Holland scheme provides interesting insights. Figure 5.2 displays graphically the initial sex differences. Girls are most interested in social and conventional jobs, and are different from the boys in this respect. The gap between the sexes is quite large, .63SD and .93SD, respectively. Girls also express an interest in artistic and enterprising jobs, but they are not different from the boys in this respect. Boys are distinguished from girls by their greater interest in realistic and investigative jobs; the gaps here are .88SD and .54SD respectively.

The target of *Freestyle*, based on this profile, should be to increase girls' interest in realistic and investigative jobs, and boys' interest in conventional and social jobs. The designers selected for girls two realistic jobs (auto mechanic, machinist), one Investigative (geologist), and two enterprising jobs (owner

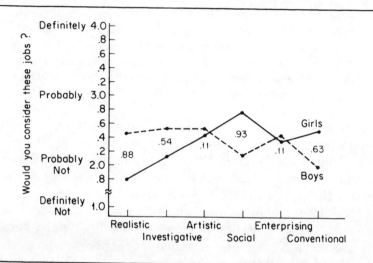

Figure 5.2 Interest in Adult Jobs: Pretest Differences for Boys and Girls (Holland Job Classifications)

of a hardware store, city council member); for boys they chose five social jobs (nurse, coach, classroom teacher, special education teacher, and occupational therapist).

Curiously, the profile suggests that enterprising jobs need not have been included. Yet in the public debate on sex equity it is access to jobs in this category that is central to the demands for gender equity. Perhaps for children of this age enterprising jobs are not visible enough to have mobilized differential interest along gender lines. Most upper elementary children may be quite unaware of the nature of such work as managing a hotel, or exercising political power in the position of city council member.

The data suggest that conventional jobs would have been a good target for boys. But their absence from the *Freestyle* arsenal is explainable on other grounds. While highly sex-typed, the designers reasoned that conventional jobs such as clerk and salesperson lack the status and reward that make them attractive alternatives. Clearly this is a judgment based on values, not strategy.

The effects of *Freestyle* on jobs in the Holland scheme are shown in Table 5.3. For each job type data are presented two ways: average interest in all the jobs in the category as well as interest in just the *Freestyle*-emphasized jobs. For example, row 1 shows average interest in the two realistic jobs shown in *Freestyle:* mechanic and machinist. Row 2 shows interest in all seven realistic jobs, including mechanic, machinist, and five other realistic jobs not portrayed in the shows. Consider first interest in the broadly defined categories. Girls' interest in realistic jobs (row 2 of Table 5.3) increased a sizable amount (.33SD), although the resulting interest level is still quite low ("probably not consider"). Girls' interest in investigative jobs was not affected at all; the shift fails to meet the criterion of minimal educational significance. For enterprising jobs the effect was just noticeable for the broadly defined category, but sizable for the two *Freestyle*-emphasized jobs. For boys the target was social jobs, and *Freestyle* had a sizable effect, .31SD. This was enough to move boys to a point midway between "probably not" and "probably;" while the meaning of this particular level of interest is ambiguous, the gap between boys' and girls' interest was reduced somewhat. Overall, categorizing adult jobs by the Holland scheme allows the detection of several modest-to-large effects on interest patterns.

Did the *Freestyle*-emphasized jobs acount for these effects? As with interest in childhood activities, the picture is mixed. With realistic and enterprising jobs for girls, shifts for the *Freestyle* jobs were larger than for the entire set of jobs; but with investigative it was the opposite — job interest increased more for investigative jobs in general than for the *Freestyle*-featured job of geologist. With social jobs for boys the effects were identical for the five *Freestyle* jobs taken separately and the complete set of nine social jobs. From these data it can only be said that the illustration of particular jobs in the *Freestyle* shows sometimes "led" the effects, but they certainly did not

TABLE 5.3 Interest in Adult Jobs by Holland Job Type

Interest in . . .	GIRLS			BOYS		
	Mean Pretest	Mean Posttest	SD Difference	Mean Pretest	Mean Posttest	SD Difference
1. Realistic (2F)[a]	1.64	2.04	.44	2.42	2.64	.24
2. Realistic (7)	1.80	2.15	.33	2.46	2.63	.23
3. Investigative (1F)	2.19	2.30	(.10)	2.62	2.69	(.06)
4. Investigative (6)	2.12	2.24	.16	2.53	2.65	(.16)
5. Artistic (2)	2.43	2.57	(.15)	2.53	2.62	(.10)
6. Social (5F)	2.81	2.89	(.11)	2.23	2.45	.30
7. Social (9)	2.77	2.86	(.13)	2.15	2.36	.31
8. Enterprising (2F)	2.16	2.46	.33	2.34	2.44	(.11)
9. Enterprising (7)	2.35	2.53	.22	2.44	2.57	.16
10. Conventional (5)	2.50	2.69	.23	1.99	2.13	(.17)

NOTE: Data are for the experimental group only. If the "SD Difference" figure is in parentheses, the experimental/control comparison was not significant at p < .05. See Chapter 4. Response scale: Definitely would = 4, probably would = 3, probably would not = 2, definitely would not = 1.

[a]There are seven "realistic" jobs on the list, of which two were emphasized in the *Freestyle* shows. The first realistic index is the average interest in the two *Freestyle* jobs; the second index the average interest in all seven realistic jobs.

carry the entire burden of change. The effects were not only specific to *Freestyle* jobs; there was generalization as well.

In sum, *Freestyle's* effects on interests are mixed. It failed to bring about a pattern of change consistent with the project's goals. But it did produce a few large changes which clearly suggest that some children did reconsider where their interests lie, although they were not totally reoriented by the experience.

To have expected greater change in interests may be un-realistic. We assessed interests with questions that required very tentative answers. "How much would you like to fix a broken bike if you had a chance," or "Would you consider becoming a car mechanic when you grow up?" As non-committal as these seem, the answers depend on "liking." Tele-vision and talk can make an activity appear attractive, but liking depends on rewards derived from trying the activity. Television is not a substitute for life.

A second reason that greater *average* change is unrealistic relates to the target for change. With beliefs or attitudes the target is appropriately *all* boys or girls, because these concepts refer to the tolerance of an entire group for the expression of nontraditional interests by the *few* who happen to be so in-clined. The target for a change in interests should be a limited number for whom the nontraditional activity is a "good fit," but who never showed their interest because they thought people of their gender did not do it (beliefs) or that theirs peers would disapprove (attitudes). In a separate analysis we found that 12 percent of the girls increased their interest in mechanical activities by a very large .50SD or more. In light of this, *Free-style* might be judged unusually effective in changing the inter-ests of a small group which was open to such change.

ALTERING BELIEFS

We have argued that the world of *Freestyle* differs from children's own world, but exposure to the world of *Freestyle* can change children's beliefs about what is true of their own. Much as we did with the interest indices, we will use the belief indices to map both the preexisting world of 9- to 12- years -olds and the effects of *Freestyle* on that world. The pretest scores show the degree to which children's own world differs from the world of *Freestyle* and also the degree to which the worlds of male and female subjects in the study differed from each other before exposure to *Freestyle*. The posttest scores, of course, reflect the impact of *Freestyle* on the world of the subjects.

Childhood Activities

Among the childhood activities emphasized in *Freestyle* we measured children's beliefs about the proportion of girls who are competent in mechanical and athetic activities and the proportion of boys who are competent in helping activities. The measures of these beliefs, like the other measures in the study, are multiple-question indices. For example, the index of beliefs about the proportion of girls who are good at mechanical activities is composed of three items:

Girls in Mechanical Activities: How many girls are good at:

(a)   fixing a broken bike?

(b)   fixing a car motor?

(c)   building a radio or something that runs on electricity?

Response choices are "all" (scored as 5), "most," "some," "a few," and "none" (scored as 1). The index was constructed by averaging the responses to these three items. The components of the other two indices are:

Girls in Athletic Activities: How many girls are good at playing:

(4a) football?

(4e) basketball?

[5 = all, 1 = none]

Boys in Helping Activities: How many boys are good at:

(5a) taking care of a younger child at the playground?

(5b) helping a child with math?

(5d) helping old people (not living in their home)?

(5e) helping an adult fix meals for the family?

[5 = all, 1 = none]

Table 5.4 presents the data for beliefs about childhood activities in tabular form, while Figure 5.3 presents in graphic form these same data plus additional information about the sex differences at both pre- and posttest. First, consider beliefs about girls in mechanical activities. Before exposure to *Freestyle,* the female subjects in our study believed that between "a few" and "some" girls are competent at mechanical activities. Males believed that only "a few" girls are good at such activities. Clearly both sexes' estimate of their own world was different from the world of *Freestyle* in which sex is unrelated to competence in mechanics or any other activity. Also, the estimates of females and males were different from each other. In standard deviation units the difference between males and females was .43SD.

Did exposure to *Freestyle* change these beliefs? Indeed it did. Both males and females changed their estimates of the proportion of girls who are good at mechanical activities to be more in line with the world of *Freestyle.* Females increased their estimate by .29SD units, and males by .44SD units. These changes not only brought the world of both sexes closer to that of *Freestyle,* but closer to each other as well. The difference between the sexes is reduced from .43SD before *Freestyle* to .27SD units afterwards.

Compare this pattern of beliefs with the one for girls in athletics. Before exposure to *Freestyle,* both male and female

TABLE 5.4 Beliefs About Childhood Activities

Beliefs about the proportion of competent . . .	FEMALES			MALES		
	Mean Pretest	Mean Posttest	SD Difference	Mean Pretest	Mean Posttest	SD Difference
Girls in mechanical activities	2.43	2.67	.29	2.07	2.44	.44
Girls in athletic activities	3.15	3.31	.17	2.55	2.84	.31
Boys in helping activities	2.70	3.06	.42	3.39	3.31	-.09

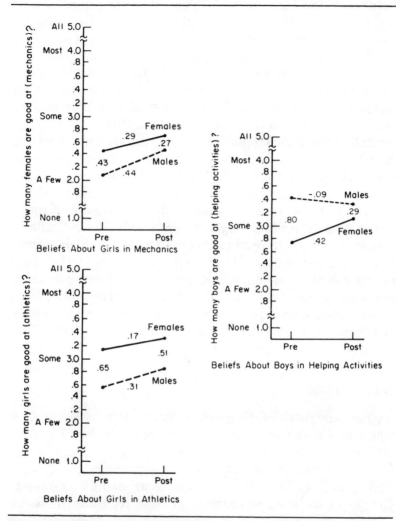

Figure 5.3   Beliefs About Childhood Activities

subjects estimated that there are more girls who are good in athletics than mechanics, but here again there is a large sex difference (.65SD units). Females estimated that slightly more than "some" girls are good at athletics, while males estimated between "a few" and "some." Even though the estimates were higher for both sexes, there was still a large difference between *Freestyle's* reality and the children's reality. What is more, the realities of male and female children were quite different.

Freestyle did, however, alter these beliefs at least for males. The increase for males was a substantial .31SD; the increase for females was .17SD. This pattern reduced the difference between males and females from .65SD to .51SD.

Beliefs about the proportion of boys who are good at helping activities shows an interesting variation on these patterns of belief. Before exposure to *Freestyle,* males estimated that between "some" and "most" boys are good at these activities. Clearly nurturing is less at odds with males' image of themselves as a group than might be imagined. The estimate of females was much lower; they believed that fewer than "some" boys are good at helping. The effect of *Freestyle* on these beliefs was to substantially increase females' lower estimates, but to moderate slightly male's higher — perhaps overinflated — estimates. With these changes the differences between male and female subjects was reduced from .80SD to .29SD. The worlds of boys and girls clearly began to converge.

Behavioral Skills

The designers of *Freestyle* believed that attainment of high-status high-paying jobs is associated with use of a set of "behavioral skills" which males are encouraged to acquire and females are not. These include leadership, independence from peer pressure, assertiveness, and reasonable risk-taking. Compared to being mechanical or athletic, these skills are complex and abstract. They are difficult to describe and even harder to symbolize in a visual medium. We measured beliefs about the competence of girls in the behavioral skills with the following indices:

Girls' Leadership Skills: How many girls are good at:

(17a) organizing things for the group to do?

(17b) giving each group member a job which they can do well?

(17d) having good ideas about what the group should do?

(17e) listening to the ideas of other group members?

[5 = all, 1 = none]

Girls' Independence Skills: How often do girls your age actually do something they're interested in:

(25a) when their friends think only boys do it?

(25b) when their parents wished they would do something else?

[5 = very often, 1 = never]

Girls' Assertiveness Skills: How many girls your age:

(26a) stand up for what they think is right?

(26b) stop somebody from picking on younger kids?

(26c) tell another kid when they think the other kid is wrong?

(26d) demand to be treated fairly by grownups?

(26e) demand to be treated fairly by other kids?

[5 = all, 1 = none]

Girls' Risk-Taking Skills: How many girls your age:

(26f) don't do things because they might get hurt doing them?

(26g) don't do things because they might be embarrassed?

(26h) try it again another way after they fail?

(26i) pick the easy thing to do instead of the hard thing?

[1 = all, 5 = none]

Table 5.5 presents the data for these indices in tabular form, while Figure 5.4 presents them in graphic form. Consider first beliefs about girls' leadership skill. Before exposure to *Freestyle,* female subjects estimated that a little less than "most" girls are good leaders. This was the highest estimate among all the behavioral skills and among all the childhood activities for that matter. For leadership, females' own world was clearly

TABLE 5.5 Beliefs About Behavioral Skills

Beliefs about the proportion of competent girls with . . .	FEMALES			MALES		
	Mean Pretest	Mean Posttest	SD Difference	Mean Pretest	Mean Posttest	SD Difference
Leadership skills	3.72	3.57	(−.17)	2.90	3.05	.18
Independence skills	3.32	3.38	.07	3.24	3.27	(.03)
Assertiveness skills	3.38	3.39	.02	3.12	3.11	(−.02)
Risk-taking skills	2.75	2.79	(.05)	2.58	2.60	(.01)

NOTE: Data are for the experimental group only. If the "SD Difference" figure is in parentheses, the experimental/control comparison was not significant at p < .05. See Chapter 4.

less at odds with the world of *Freestyle* than for any other concept examined in our research. The male subjects did not share the female's view, however. Males estimated that fewer than "some" girls are good leaders. Here again, as with beliefs about childhood activities, there was a major difference between the worlds of boys and girls before *Freestyle*.

After exposure to *Freestyle,* the changes in beliefs presented a pattern very much like the changes in beliefs about boys' nurturing activities, where the sex with the lower initial estimate significantly increased its estimate after exposure to *Freestyle* while the sex with the higher initial estimate revised its estimate downwards. In the case of beliefs about girls' leadership skills, male subjects increased their lower initial estimate by .18SD units while female subjects reduced their initially very high estimates by an almost equal amount. The world of the males thus became more like both the world of *Freestyle* and the world of the females in the study. Here again *Freestyle* has shown at least some success in altering sex-role perceptions. The pattern suggests that it operates to reduce a kind of "sexual chauvinism" that sometimes exist.

The results for the other three indices of beliefs about girls' behavioral skills disrupts this pattern of success, however. For girls behaving independently of peer pressure, female and male subjects both said before *Freestyle* that girls do not behave this way very often. After exposure to the series neither sex changed significantly. For the girls' assertiveness and risk-taking, both male and female subjects said that "some" girls are skilled; but again, after exposure to the series neither sex raised its estimate.

Overall, *Freestyle's* impact on beliefs about behavioral skills is much less impressive than its impact on beliefs about childhood activities. For only one of the four indices and then for only male subjects did *Freestyle* achieve effects which meet the test of significance we have adopted. Clearly there are limits to *Freestyle's* power to shape or reshape children's perceptions of reality.

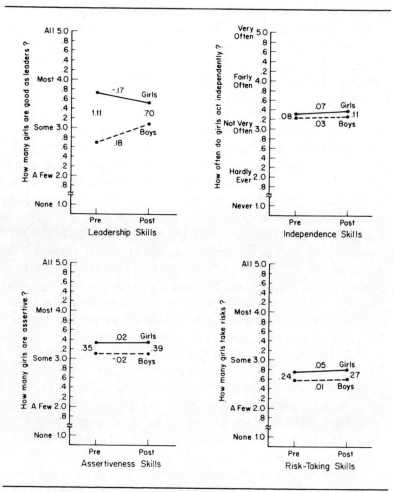

Figure 5.4 Beliefs About Girls' Behavioral Skills

Adult Roles

We measured six beliefs about adult work and family roles: beliefs about the proportion of men and women who occupy traditionally male and female jobs, the amount of traditionally male household work done by wives and traditionally female household work done by husbands and, finally, the extent to which wives and husbands earn money to support the family.

Adult Work Roles. The items measuring beliefs about work roles are shown below; the data and corresponding graphs appear in Table 5.6 and Figure 5.5.

Proportion of Men and Women in Traditionally Male Jobs: How many of the people who do each of these jobs are men and how many are women:

(7a) car mechanic?

(7b) truck driver?

(7e) machinist (makes parts for machines)?

(7f) pharmacist (gives out medicine in a drugstore)?

(7g) owner of a hardware store?

(7h) city council member (someone elected to run a city)?

(7i) geologist (scientist who studies rocks and minerals)?

(7j) worker in a factory who puts things together (like a car)?

(7l) sales person in a store who sells cars or TVs or refrigerators?

[5 = all women, 1 = all men]

Proportion of Men and Women in Traditionally Female Jobs: How many of the people who do each of these jobs are men and how many are women:

(7c) nurse?

(7d) secretary?

(7k) telephone operator?

(7o) dental assistant (cleans people's teeth or helps dentist fix their teeth?

(7p) teacher of children who have problems with seeing or hearing?

(7q) occupational therapist (help sick or old people learn new skills)?

[5 = all women, 1 = all men]

TABLE 5.6 Beliefs About Adult Roles

MEASURE	FEMALES			MALES		
	Mean Pretest	Mean Posttest	SD Difference	Mean Pretest	Mean Posttest	SD Difference
Belief about the proportion of men and women in . . .						
Traditionally male jobs	2.31	2.46	.39	2.15	2.30	.39
Traditionally female jobs	3.81	3.64	−.33[a]	3.81	3.62	−.37[a]
Belief about the proportion of . . .						
Wives doing traditionally male household tasks	2.52	2.78	.27	2.27	2.50	.24
Husbands doing traditionally female household tasks	2.46	2.78	.39	2.51	2.69	.22
Wives earning money to support the family	2.46	2.48	.02	2.83	2.80	(−.03)
Husbands earning money to support the family	4.22	4.20	(−.02)	4.37	4.24	(−.15)

NOTE: Data are for the experimental group only. If the "SD Difference" figure is in parentheses, the experimental/control comparison was not significant at p < .05. See Chapter 4.

[a]Wording of question makes negative value desirable.

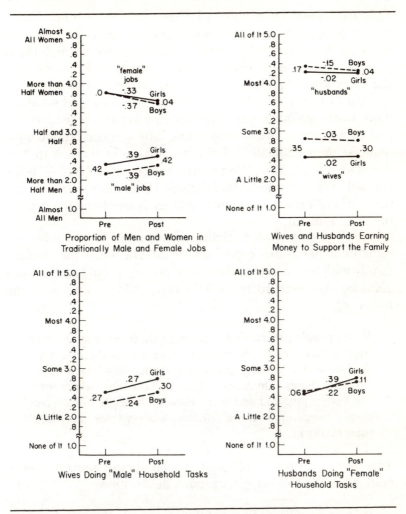

Figure 5.5 Beliefs About Adult Men and Women in Adult Roles

With children's beliefs about the sex of those in traditionally male and female jobs *Freestyle* is once again successful. Before exposure to *Freestyle,* girls and boys agreed that "more than half" of those who hold traditionally male jobs are, in fact, men;

and that "more than half" of those who hold traditionally female jobs are women. Before *Freestyle,* then, the girls and boys in the study were alike in their estimates; and these estimates, no doubt, correlated more strongly with the reality of the labor force than with reality in the world of *Freestyle.*

After *Freestyle,* however, boys and girls changed substantially. Both significantly increased their estimates of the proportion of women in traditionally male jobs and correspondingly reduced their estimates of the proportion of women in traditionally female jobs. With these changes all children — boys and girls alike — brought their beliefs a little more into line with the world of *Freestyle* in which gender is unrelated to occupational attainment.

Adult Family Roles. Beliefs about adult family roles are difficult to measure, especially in an era when the nuclear family with both a husband and wife present is not familiar to all children. To standardize the stimulus, children were read the following:

> When people get married, they must do things such as earn money, take care of children, and take care of things around the house. The husband and wife must decide who is going to do these things. Think about families you know where there are both a husband and wife. How do husbands and wives divide things up in these families? (Don't think just about your family.)

This introduction was followed by a number of questions summarized in the following four index descriptions.

Proportion of Wives Doing Male Housework: How much is done by wives today:

(10a) take care of things around the house (paint the house fix leaky faucets)?

(10b) take care of the car (keep it clean, have the oil changed)?

[5 = all of it, 1 = none of it]

Proportion of Husbands Doing Female Housework: How much is done by husbands today:

(10d) grocery shopping, cook the meals, do the dishes?

(10e) do the house cleaning (dust, vacuum, scrub the floors, clean the bathroom)?

(10f) take care of the children?

[5 = all of it, 1 = none of it]

Wives Who Earn Money to Support the Family:

(10c) How much do wives work to earn money to support the family?

[5 = none, 1 = all]

Husbands Who Earn Money to Support the Family:

(10g) How much do husbands work to earn money to support the family?

[5 = all, 1 = none]

The results for beliefs about household tasks are similar to those for occupations. Before exposure to *Freestyle,* girls said that wives did between "a little" and "some" of the traditionally male household work and that husbands did about the same amount of traditionally female work. Boys agreed with girls about the amount of nontraditional work done by husbands but thought that the anount done by wives was somewhat less than the girls had estimated.

After *Freestyle,* both boys and girls increased their estimates of the amount of nontraditional household work done by husbands and wives. The gap between boys and girls remained, but here again *Freestyle* moved the beliefs of all children more into line with its own reality.

Freestyle was less successful changing beliefs about who earns money to support the family. Before exposure to *Freestyle,* girls estimated that between "a little" and "some" of the support comes from wives while boys estimated that it was somewhat higher. Conversely, girls estimated that between "most" and "all" of this work is done by husbands while boys estimated that it was a little higher. With the recent dramatic increase in the number of working wives these beliefs correlate with neither the reality of labor statistics nor the reality of *Freestyle*. After exposure to the series, there was little change for either of these beliefs for either sex.

The Limits of *Freestyle's* Influence

The world of *Freestyle* was created to be a coherent, compelling but different reality. It is now clear that exposure to this world changed some of what children believe to be true about their own world. The data show that one or both sexes reevaluated the competence of children in several nontraditional pre-occupational activities. Both sexes also reestimated the proportion of men and women in various jobs and family roles. Some of these changes made the differing worlds of boys and girls more alike; all of the changes made the worlds of the subjects more like the nonstereotyped world of *Freestyle*. Beliefs are, then, an aspect of children's lives which is open to the influence of the *Freestyle* experience.

Our data have also shown, however, that not all of the measured beliefs were affected. Exposure to *Freestyle* did not change either sex's estimate of the proportion of family financial support contributed by husbands and wives. Nor did it change either sex's estimate of the competence of girls in three of the four behavioral skills: independence, assertiveness, and risk-taking. *Freestyle's* power to shape the reality of its audience is definitely not unlimited.

Analysis of the limits to *Freestyle's* influence must, for now, be speculative, but two general ideas suggest themselves. One idea is to look to the audience; the other is to look to *Freestyle* itself. *Freestyle's* inability to alter beliefs about who works to support the family may, for example, reflect limits imposed by *Freestyle* itself. The working women most vividly portrayed in the series were not ordinary breadwinners; rather they were individuals who rose to meet challenging circumstances. Penny's mom, who runs a hardware store, assumed the job upon the death of her husband. Walter and Tess's mom took a job outside the home when her husband suddenly became unemployed. Children may have viewed these women as exceptional and seen no reason to change their minds about who, in general, works to support the family.

On the other hand, *Freestyle's* inability to change these beliefs may reflect limits imposed by the audience. The work-lives of parents are an organizing feature of children's lives. Their experience with their own families may support and maintain their beliefs about all families. Beliefs about who works to support the family would, then, be both highly salient and solidly anchored in personal experience. Such beliefs would be difficult to change. Similarly, *Freestyle's* inability to alter beliefs about the competence of girls in several behavioral skills could reflect limits imposed by the audience. It is difficult to imagine, however, why these particular beliefs would be more solidly anchored in personal experience than, say, beliefs about girls' mechanical or athletic abilities. It seems more likely in this case that we have definitely found limits imposed by the messages. This idea comes to us from the *Freestyle* developers themselves. They realized that some of the messages could be more easily communicated in a dramatic series than others. They knew that competence in such concrete activities as athletics could be portrayed in a single visual image. So too could the presence of men and women in nontraditional work and family roles. When a girl scores the winning touchdown or a woman takes command of a huge machine the point is forcefully made. The competence of children in abstract behavioral skills, on the other hand, is not so easily portrayed. Complex stories, not simple images, are necessary to make the point.

The *Freestyle* developers tried to make the messages about behavioral skills as comprehensible to their young audience as possible. In particular, the device of the Ah-ha! scene was invented so that the messages embedded in the stories could be verbalized by the characters and made explicit. As we saw in Chapter 3, however, this device was not consistently success-ful. Indeed, the episode concerning risk-taking was the least well understood of the three episodes singled out for study in that chapter. The risk-taking message, and other behavioral skills messages as well, remained beyond the reach of the children for whom they were intended.

Our argument is, in essence, that some beliefs are difficult to change with television drama and others are simply difficult to change. The idea that some beliefs are solidly anchored in personal experience is supported by a generation of communi-cated research. Time and again researchers have found that individuals' social relationships and experiences shape and limit the effects of mass communication upon them.[2] The idea that other beliefs are difficult to change because messages about them are too complex and abstract to be effectively communicated to children by television drama does not have such research support. The idea does, however, have the sup-port of the very people who scripted those messages. A number of the script writers, all seasoned Hollywood professionals, said that it was difficult to both tell a good story and work in the messages specified in the curriculum — particularly messages about behavioral skills. They argued that effective drama deals more with emotions than abstract ideas and that *Freestyle's* complex prosocial messages often were not amenable to dra-matic presentation.

The findings of researchers and the judgments of television professionals suggest that the pattern of *Freestyle's* influence reflects fundamental limits to the influence of any television series on the beliefs of its audience. Before these limits are too firmly drawn, however, we must acknowledge that our indices tap only a limited range of sex-role beliefs. When these meas-ures are supplemented by the face-to-face interviews employed in the Ann Arbor research site, it is clear that the effects of

Freestyle are not necessarily limited to the simple, concrete, and easily dramatized.

In Ann Arbor, we asked children to explain why individuals do not engage in certain nontraditional pursuits and why they may not be competent in them. Children's answers to the question: "Why don't girls play football more than they do?" are summarized in Table 5.7. Consider in particular the answers of the male subjects. All of the males in the control group said that girls do not play by their own choice. They maintained that girls do not play because they are afraid of getting hurt, or because they think it is a game only for boys, or simply because they do not like it. On the other hand, among males in the treatment group, only 65 percent said that girls do not play more by their own choice. Another 23 percent explained the situation with reference to the attitudes and behaviors of boys. They mentioned teasing and other barriers to participation as an explanation of girls' behavior. This same pattern of answers was repeated for questions about why girls do not engage in mechanical activities, why men do not become nurses, and why women do not work unloading trucks more than they do. Thus, *Freestyle* — the series along with class discussion — showed at least some children, especially males, that sex roles are not necessarily a matter of personal preference, that there are barriers to expanded sex roles, and that they themselves help to erect those barriers. In short, *Freestyle* provided an alternative explanation for why things are as they are. This is an effect of considerable subtlety and power, an effect which makes us reluctant to draw too firmly the limits to *Freestyle's* influence, or that of prosocial television in general.

CHANGING ATTITUDES

Beliefs may be solidly anchored in personal experience, and this may limit the amount that beliefs can be changed. But what about attitudes — the approval or disapproval which one feels toward the ways in which other people behave? This "affect"

TABLE 5.7 Children's Responses to "Why don't girls play football more than they do?"

Category of response	MALES		FEMALES	
	Control	Treatment	Control	Treatment
Girl's own preference	100.0% (25)	65.2% (45)	72.2% (31)	63.3% (52)
Boy's attitude or behavior	0.0% (0)	23.2% (16)	25.6% (11)	34.2% (28)
Other responses	0.0% (0)	11.6% (8)	2.3% (1)	2.4% (2)
TOTALS	100.0% (25)	100.0% (69)	100.0% (43)	100.0% (82)

may be rooted in experience and in the subtle reactions of parents and peers, but it may be less firmly anchored. Reality impinges on the consciousness daily; the sources of affect are less frequently encountered.

We measured attitudes by asking respondents whether they considered it a good idea for boys or girls to do various activities considered nontraditional for their sex. Using this approach it might be more accurate to describe our measures as norms. By either term such measures are relevant in evaluating an intervention such as *Freestyle*. Individuals act in a social context. Their behaviors are influenced to some extent by the norm, or perceived norms, for such behavior. Thus it is hard to imagine a girl trying out for a touch football team if she feels that all her "significant others" would disapprove. Put more positively, it is easier to imagine increased numbers of girls choosing touch football if girls perceive that such behavior is approved by others. Accordingly, we measured children's attitudes toward nontraditional sex-role behavior because it reflects the perceived norms for such behavior. If *Freestyle* can shift these norms, it can alter the climate in ways which can increase the likelihood that nontraditional behavior will occur.

Childhood Activities

Sex-role attitudes about pre-occupational activities were measured as follows.

Girls in Mechanics: How do you feel about girls your age:

(2b) fixing a broken bike?

(2c) working with an adult on a car motor?

(2d) building a radio or something else that runs on electricity?

[4 = very good idea, 1 = very bad idea]

Girls in Athletics: How do you feel about girls your age:

(2a) playing football on a team with both boys and girls on the team?

(2e) playing basketball on a team with boys and girls on the team?
[4 = very good idea, 1 = very bad idea]

Boys in Helping Roles: How do you feel about boys:
(3a) taking care of a younger child at the playground?
(3b) helping a child with math?
(3d) helping old people (not living in their home)?
(3e) helping an adult fix meals for the family?
[4 = very good idea, 1 = very bad idea]

Note first the range of "support" for the various activities at the time of the pretest (Table 5.8 and Figure 5.6). The pretest data show children's norms before exposure to *Freestyle;* they also help us ascribe meaning to the scales we have used to measure those norms. Before exposure, the lowest average support was expressed by males regarding girls doing mechanical or athletic activities. The scores of 2.38 and 2.47 are halfway between "good idea" and "bad idea." We saw in the previous section of this chapter that males thought only "a few" girls were good at these same mechanical activities, and that only "a few girls were good at athletics. These and other considerations lead us to define the portion of the scale between 2.30 and 2.60 as an area of moderate disapproval.

The next highest level of approval was the response of females to girls doing mechanical activities — 2.73. We saw that females showed very little interest in doing mechanical activities, and believed that only slightly more than "a few" girls are good at such activities. In contrast, females' attitude toward girls in athletics was 3.08, right at the scale point of "good idea." We saw that females showed much more interest in athletics than mechanics, and that they believed more girls were good at athletic endeavors than at mechanics. These and similar observations lead us to treat average responses in the 2.70 to 2.90 range as indicating low but positive approval of the

TABLE 5.8   Attitudes Regarding Children in Nontraditional Activities

Attitude toward . . .	FEMALES				MALES		
	Mean Pretest	Mean Posttest	SD Difference	Mean Pretest	Mean Posttest	SD Difference	
Girls in mechanical activities	2.73	3.14	.48	2.38	2.84	.53	
Girls in athletics	3.08	3.47	.41	2.47	2.92	.47	
Boys in helping activities	2.95	3.33	.55	3.03	3.22	.28	

NOTE: Data are for the experimental group only. If the "SD Difference" figure is in parentheses, the experimental/control comparison was not significant at $p < .05$. See Chapter 4.

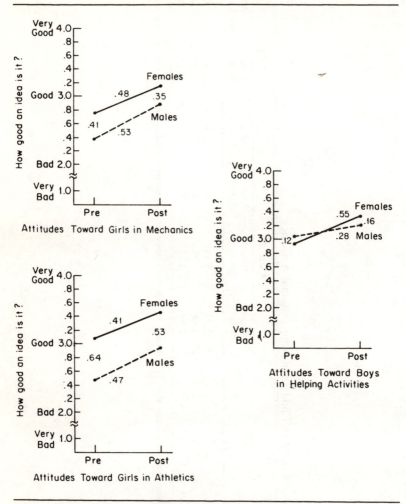

Figure 5.6 Attitudes About Childhood Activities

behavior, and ratings in the range of 3.00 to 3.20 indicating moderate approval. Very strong approval is associated with average responses of 3.30 to 3.50.

After exposure to *Freestyle,* children's norms regarding girls in mechanical and athletic activities show a very large change. The increase for both males and females ranges from .41SD to .53SD. Males moved from a position of disapproval to low but positive approval. For females, approval of girls in mechanical activities increased from low to moderate approval, and approval of girls in athletics increased from moderate to strong. Approval of boys in helping activities increased very dramatically for females. The increase for males was less dramatic, but positive nonetheless. The *Freestyle* experience is clearly associated with large and dramatic effects for nontraditional childhood activities.

Behavioral Skills

Freestyle's effects on attitudes regarding behavioral skills was much smaller and more complicated. The attitudes were assessed with these indices:

Girls in Leadership Roles: How do you feel about girls:

(16a) being president of your class?

(16b) being captain of your school's football team?

(16c) being in charge of your class paper drive and giving orders to the other kids?

(16d) being editor in charge of the school newspaper?

[4 = very good idea, 1 = very bad idea]

Girls Showing Independence: How would you feel if a girl your age did something she was interested in doing:

(23a) when her close friends wanted her to do something else with them?

(23b) when her close friends thought it was a thing only boys should do?

(23c) when her parents wished she would do something else?

[4 = very good idea, 1 = very bad idea]

Girls Being Assertive:

(30)   How good an idea is it for a girl your age to try to stop a kid your age from picking on a little kid rather than getting the teacher?

(32)   How good an idea is it for a girl who plays the saxophone very well to try to go to the teacher and prove that she's good enough despite the fact that there are already enough saxophones in the band?

[4 = very good idea, 1 = very bad idea]

Girls Taking Risks: How do you feel about a girl:

(35a) raising her hand in class when she is not sure of the answer?

(35b) taking apart a bike to fix it when she is not sure how to do it?

(35c) trying to bake cookies using a recipe that is much harder than she has used before?

(35d) trying a new sport when she is not sure she can do it well?

(35e) climbing onto a high place where she's not sure she can get down?

[4 = very good idea, 1 = very bad idea]

To provide an anchor against which to judge the norms for girls, norms for boys were also assessed. Identical items were used, changing only the stem to "how do you feel about boys . . . ?"

The strongest and clearest effects were found for independence. The norms for girls and boys behaving independently are shown in rows 5 and 6 of Table 5.9. Before *Freestyle,* males and females alike were modestly disapproving of either sex displaying an independent streak. *Freestyle* had a sizable effect on this norm for all children, increasing approval of independent behavior by one-third to two-fifths of a standard deviation to a level of low approval. This effect on norms for both sexes mirrors the treatment of independence in the *Freestyle* series. The episode focusing on independence ("Cheers!") features both a boy and a girl who resist pressure from their respective peer groups. Penny is good at cheerleading and Ramon at

TABLE 5.9   Attitudes Regarding Children Exercising Nontraditional Behavioral Skills

	FEMALES			MALES		
Attitudes toward . . . [a]	Mean Pretest	Mean Posttest	SD Difference	Mean Pretest	Mean Posttest	SD Difference
Girls being leaders (LB)	3.17	3.33	.20	2.25	2.58	.42
Girls being leaders (MIL)	3.17	3.21	(.05)	2.04	2.32	.33
Boys being leaders (LB)	2.96	3.20	.38	3.52	3.42	(−.16)
Boys being leaders (MIL)	2.80	3.03	.32	3.52	3.41	(−.15)
Girls showing independence (LB)	2.62	2.86	.36	2.56	2.83	.40
Boys showing independence (LB)	2.55	2.79	.39	2.57	2.75	.30
Girls being assertive (LB)	2.26	2.52	.34	2.23	2.43	.25
Girls being assertive (MIL)	2.50	2.56	(.05)	2.39	2.41	(.02)
Girls taking risks (LB)	2.21	2.19	(−.03)	2.14	2.21	(.12)
Boys taking risks (LB)	2.20	2.21	(.02)	2.27	2.34	(.12)

NOTE: Data are for the experimental group only. If the "SD Difference" figure is in parentheses, the experimental/control comparison was not significant at p < .05. See Chapter 4.

[a]LB = data from Long Beach; MIL = data from Milwaukee.

soccer; both of them are also interested in science. To pursue a science fair project they must give up their athletic ativities to gain time to work on the project. Penny's teammates on the cheerleading squad and Ramon's on the soccer team pressure them to remain on the teams, but Penny and Ramon display their independence and resign. Both sexes displayed independence, and this seems to have had the effect of increasing approval of independent behavior for both sexes.

The picture for leadership is more complicated. The first four rows of Table 5.9 show attitudes in both Long Beach and Milwaukee toward girls and boys being leaders. Before *Freestyle,* males were highly approving of boys in leadership positions such as class president, paper drive chairman, and so forth, but they were quite disapproving of girls in these positions. *Freestyle* enhanced males' approval of girl leaders (.42SD in Long Beach and .33SD in Milwaukee), although after the series they were still modestly disapproving (2.58 in Long Beach and 2.32 in Milwaukee). *Freestyle* decreased males' enthusiasm for boy leaders by a small amount as though their original approval had been a bit "puffed up." Females, on the other hand, started out quite approving of girls as leaders (3.17 in both cities) and almost as approving of boys as leaders. *Freestyle* increased their approval of girls but not by an educationally significant amount; and it increased their approval of boys as leaders by a very large amount (.32SD and .38SD). *Freestyle* clearly "shook up" all the norms regarding leadership. But the most relevant norm is males' disapproval of girls as leaders. As noted, *Freestyle* had a sizable effect, but it only moved males to a less *dis*approving level.

The data for risk-taking are shown in the last two rows of Table 5.9. Before *Freestyle,* neither males nor females approved of girls taking risks and *Freestyle* was unable to change this norm. There is a similar pattern regarding boys' risk-taking. *Freestyle's* failure here might rest with the resilience of the norm or with *Freestyle* itself. The "risk-taking" show was an episode called "Hike" which, as we observed in an earlier chapter, was understood by very few viewers. Most viewers thought the show's message was to stay with the leader when you go on a hike!

"Homogenization"

Differential change for certain subgroups provide interesting insights into the dynamics of attitude change. In Long Beach before *Freestyle* white and black students were approving of girls acting independently; Mexican-Americans, however, were quite disapproving. After *Freestyle,* the attitudes of Mexican-Americans were almost identical with other groups. In Milwaukee, a similar phenomenon occurred, only with different subgroups. Here Hispanics and whites were similar in approving girls' independent behavior, but Blacks were less supportive. After *Freestyle,* the attitudes of Blacks were quite close to the other two groups. In Worcester, Blacks started out less approving than whites but changed in the course of *Freestyle* to a level identical with whites. Perhaps it is the minority role model of Ramon in the show "Cheers"; perhaps it is the opportunity for disparate groups to discuss the issues in a common setting of the classroom (all classrooms with minorities had both whites and minorities in them). Whatever the explanation, it leads us to identify a type of effect which we call "homogenization."

A variation of this effect is seen for assertiveness (rows 7 and 8 of Table 5.9). Consider first the norms in Long Beach for girls being assertive. Before *Freestyle,* both males and females disapproved of assertive behavior in girls. *Freestyle* had modest to sizable effects on this norm although the resulting ratings were still at a level of "modest *dis*approval." Milwaukee children were initially much more supportive than those in Long Beach, and there was no change after *Freestyle.* The Milwaukee posttest scores were almost identical to those in Long Beach. It may be that there are national norms regarding approval of the kinds of assertive behavior measured in the index.

If a group or site is below that norm, the *Freestyle* experience raises it up to the limit.

In sum, *Freestyle* was fairly successful altering norms for girls displaying independence, less successful for girls exercising leadership and assertiveness, and not at all successful with risk-taking. Compared to its effects on *beliefs* about behavioral skills, *Freestyle* was more successful.

Adult Roles

The acceptability of women in male jobs was measured by these items:

Women in Male Jobs: How would you feel if more women were:

(8a) car mechanics?

(8b) truck drivers?

(8c) machinists (make parts for machines)?

(8d) owners of hardware stores?

(8e) geologists (scientists who study rocks and minerals)?

[4 = very good idea, 1 = very bad idea]

These jobs were chosen to represent some of the most sextyped jobs in society — jobs which were all illustrated in the *Freestyle* series. Table 5.10 presents the data. Boys in the study were disapproving of women in male jobs; but the *Freestyle* experience changed this by a very large amount — .55SD — to a point of low approval (2.76). While girls in the study were more approving to begin with (2.87), they also increased their acceptance by a sizable .32SD.

The index of the acceptability of men in female jobs is composed of three jobs:

Men in Female Jobs: How would you feel if more men were:

(9a) nurses?

TABLE 5.10 Attitudes Toward Men and Women in Nontraditional Adult Roles

Attitudes toward . . .	GIRLS			BOYS		
	Mean Pretest	Mean Posttest	SD Difference	Mean Pretest	Mean Posttest	SD Difference
More women in male jobs[a]	2.87	3.08	.32	2.40	2.76	.55
More men in female jobs[a]	2.77	3.17	.58	2.46	2.87	.59
Wives doing male housework[b]	2.43	2.84	.41	2.36	2.62	.26
Husbands doing female housework[b]	2.76	3.06	.33	2.52	2.88	.40
Wives supporting the family[b]	2.32	2.39	.06	2.98	3.10	.10
Husbands supporting the family[b]	4.25	4.07	-.19	4.24	4.14	-.10

NOTE: Data are for the experimental group only. If the "SD Difference" figure is in parentheses, the experimental/control comparison was not significant at p < .05. See chapter 4.

[a] 4 = very good idea; 1 = very bad idea.
[b] 5 = should do all of it; 1 = should do none of it.

(9b) teachers of children who have problems with seeing or hearing?

(9c) occupational therapists (help sick or old people learn new skills)?

[4 = very good idea, 1 = very bad idea]

On the average, boys in the study were modestly disapproving of men engaging in these jobs (2.47); but this average score was due almost entirely to their strong feelings against men being nurses. Their response of 1.60 is midway between a "very bad idea" and "a bad idea." Boys showed low but positive approval (2.89) of men in the other two female jobs. The job of nurse is perhaps among the most sex-typed in our society. To say "nurse" is to imply "woman." In light of this it is perhaps all the more striking that *Freestyle* had a very strong effect on the norms for men in female jobs. The large effect for the complete index (.59SD) is due mostly to an extremely large shift in favor of men being nurses: from 1.60 to 2.46, a shift of .85SD. Girls also increased their approval by a very large amount, but they were not as strongly opposed initially as were the boys in the study.

For family roles a different question prototype was used, since the issue here is husbands and wives sharing household chores. The questions were:

Wives Doing Male Housework: How much do you think each of these things should be done by wives:

(11a) take care of things around the house (paint the house, fix leaking faucets)?

(11b) take care of the car (keep it clean, have the oil changed)?

[5 = all of it, 1 = none of it]

Husbands Doing Female Housework: How much do you think each of these things should be done by husbands:

(11d) do the grocery shopping, cook the meals, do the dishes?

(11e) do the housecleaning (dust, vacuum, scrub the floors, clean the bathroom?

(11f) take care of the children?

[5 = all of it, 1 = none of it]

Wives Supporting the Family: How much of the money to support the family should be earned by the wife?

[5 = all of it, 1 = none of it]

Husbands Supporting the Family: How much of the money to support the family should be earned by the husband?

[5 = all of it, 1 = none of it]

Initially boys in the study were modestly disapproving of either husbands or wives doing the household tasks that are traditionally the responsibility of the other sex. The *Freestyle* experience changed boys' norms, especially those concerning husbands doing female housework (.40SD). The shift was from modest disapproval to low but positive approval. Girls in the study were also affected and by "sizable" to "very large" amounts.

The shift toward greater approval of husbands doing female housework is critical when it comes to expanding sex roles in society. Without males sharing the female tasks it is very difficult to create a situation in which women can establish satisfying careers outside the home. Even more critical, however, are norms supporting the family, and *Freestyle* was notably unsuccessful in changing these norms (rows 5 and 6, Table 5.10). Overall, *Freestyle* shows the capability to dramatically change many sex-role norms of children. Some norms are resistant to change, but it is unclear whether this is attributable to the nature of the norm or failings in *Freestyle's* treatment.

The effect sizes for attitudes were larger, on the average, than those for beliefs. This suggests that attitudes are indeed less firmly anchored and more amenable to change by a television-based intervention. In the next section on the persistence of effects we will see additional evidence in support of this.

NINE MONTHS LATER: THE PERSISTENCE OF EFFECTS

The data from the validation study of *Freestyle* indicate that *Freestyle* is indeed capable of bringing about large changes in the sex-role orientation of 9- to 12-year-olds. But were these just fleeting feelings created by an exceptional school experience? Would they disappear after children had a chance to check some of their new ideas against the realities and norms of their own world? To investigate, we collected a third wave of data in one of the experimental cities.

The Persistence Study

During a three-week period in the fall of 1979, a third wave of data was collected from students in nine elementary and four junior high schools in Ann Arbor. We believe that the *Freestyle* intervention was essentially absent in the nine months that separated the second and third waves. During the first four of those months children continued in the same classrooms, but without *Freestyle*. Then there was summer vacation and two months in new classrooms as the next school year began. Students who were sixth graders during the experiment moved to totally new buildings as well. In a few cases, some of the teachers who were in the original experiment were the new teachers for the previous fourth and fifth grade students, but this was true for less than 20 percent of the students. The period between the original posttest in February 1979, and the "post-post" test in November 1979 was, then, a time when *Freestyle* was not an integral part of these children's lives.

The questionnaire used to collect the third wave of data was identical to the one used for the pretest and posttest in the Ann Arbor site. It differed slightly from the one used in other sites because it included only a subset of the questions. This was done to reduce the burden on students in Ann Arbor who were asked to complete not only a paper-and-pencil questionnaire, but an extensive interview as well. As it turned out, this subset of questions included the content areas in which the largest initial effects were detected: beliefs and attitudes regarding pre-occupational activities and leadership as well as beliefs and attitudes about adult work roles.

In Ann Arbor, 589 students had completed both pre- and posttests. The third-wave questionnaire was completed by 78 percent of these students. When the students who "persisted" through all three waves were compared with the "dropouts," two things were found. Within the experimental group, persisters were almost identical to dropouts in their demographic characteristics and in their initial scores on the indices of interest to us. The same was not true within the control group. Students who persisted looked quite different from the original control group. Accordingly, the data in this section are presented for only the experimental group persisters who were in classrooms where *Freestyle* was implemented fully. We are comfortable with this decision; the control group had shown no movement on these measures between the pretest and posttest, so it seems reasonable to assume that the controls would not have shifted between the posttest and post-posttest either.

In the exploration of effects discussed thus far, an estimate of the size of effect was made by dividing the raw pre-to-post gain score by the standard deviation of the pretest data. An extension of this same strategy permits talking about persistence of effects in the same metric. This time, however, the raw gain from Time 2 to Time 3 is divided by the pretest standard deviation. An example may be useful here. Look at the Ann Arbor portion of Figure 5.7 which presents the data on attitudes toward girls in mechanical activities. Boys' attitudes increased from 2.64 to 3.01 from pretest to posttest. When divided by the pretest standard deviation (.78) for boys and girls combined, this translates to a .47SD increase. The boys' scores at the time

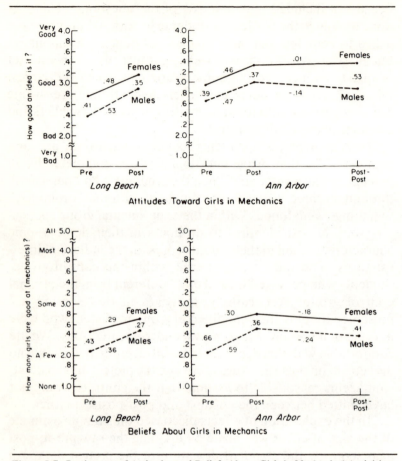

Figure 5.7 Persistence of Attitudes and Beliefs About Girls in Mechanical Activities

of the post-posttest averaged 2.90. Subtracting 2.90 from 3.01 and dividing by the same pretest standard deviation of .78, this converts to a decline of −.14SD.

In analyzing the data on persistence of effects we present the corresponding beliefs and attitudes together. This facilitates comparisons of persistence for beliefs and attitudes across the various content areas. In each figure we show the pre/post data for Long Beach as well. Since Ann Arbor as a site was slightly more restricted in both sample size and demographics (for example, there were no Hispanics), the juxtaposition permits a most interesting comparison. In most cases the Ann Arbor sample prior to *Freestyle* was very similar to Long Beach in its sex-role orientation, and the pre/post effects were also very similar. Thus, although persistence of effects was studied only in Ann Arbor, this cross-site comparison increases our confidence that the dynamics are representative of what might have happened in other sites as well. Our presentation will be with graphs; but Table C.2 in Appendix C presents for all the outcomes both cross-time SD shifts and the decay as a percentage of initial effect.

The Persistence of Effects

Girls in Mechanical Activities. Figure 5.7 presents the data for beliefs and attitudes concerning girls in mechanical activities. For attitudes, the pre-to-post increase of .46SD for female subjects and .47SD for males indicates *Freestyle* was very persuasive. Since there was no corresponding movement for the control group, we can conclude that *Freestyle* alone accounts for this shift. The persistence data for female respondents indicate that the attitude effect does not decay during the subsequent nine months. For male respondents the effect decays somewhat (−.14SD). This decay corresponds to 30 percent of the initial effect (.14/.47). Another way of looking at it is that the net gain for boys from the *Freestyle* intervention is .33SD (.47SD − .14SD) over a 13-month period. This would still be a sizable effect to attribute to an intervention such as this.

On the negative side, however, the trend lines suggest that across time the gap between boys' and girls' attitudes is widening. This could eventually inhibit girls' interest in mechanical activities.

Beliefs about whether girls are good at mechanical pursuits were strongly influenced by the orginal *Freestyle* intervention

(bottom of Figure 5.7). Female subjects increased their estimate of the number of girls with mechanical ability by .30SD,
and males increased their estimate by a very large .59SD. For
females, however, there was a 60 percent decay and for males a
41 percent decay over the nine months subsequent to *Freestyle,*
which is larger than the decay in the corresponding attitude,
especially for girls. It seems *Freestyle* and the accompanying
classroom activities present a view of girls which does not stand
the test of time well. Perhaps, for example, the image of Chris
successfully repairing the car in the show " Grease Monkey"
was very vivid in children's minds at the time of the posttest,
but subsequently the image was deemed atypical. However,
while the beliefs undergo a readjustment, females' and males'
perceptions are closer together at the time of the final data
collection than at the first one.

Girls in Athletics. In Long Beach, *Freestyle* had a very
strong effect on attitudes toward girls in athletics. Long Beach
female subjects changed more than Ann Arbor females, but in
Long Beach the scores were much lower to begin with (3.08 for
Long Beach females versus 3.43 for Ann Arbor females). Both
Long Beach and Ann Arbor females at posttest time were very
high in approval (3.47 for Long Beach and 3.61 for Ann Arbor).
Figure 5.8 shows that there was some decay of attitudes toward
girls' participation in athletics — a decline of one-third of the
initial effect for girls and one-fourth of the initial effect for boys.

In regard to beliefs about how many girls are good at football or basketball, *Freestyle* had convinced male subjects that
at least "some" girls are capable. It was even more effective at
this in Ann Arbor than Long Beach, but this effect decayed
considerably. The initial effect of .59SD for boys was followed
by a −.25SD decline. This decline is 42 percent of the original
effect. The much smaller initial effect for females (.19SD) decayed by 37 per cent. Here again the decay in beliefs is greater
than for the corresponding attitudes.

Boys in helping activities. At the time of the pretest females
and males were both supportive of boys doing such things as

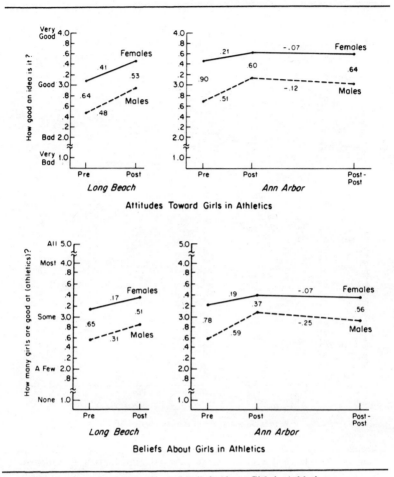

Figure 5.8 Persistence of Attitudes and Beliefs About Girls in Athletics

taking care of a younger child, helping a child with math, helping older people, and helping adults fix meals for the family. Despite the high level of initial support, *Freestyle* enhanced these attitudes: .46SD for males and .43SD or females (Figure 5.9). But for males there was almost total decay — 89 percent of the original effect. For females the decay was 30 percent

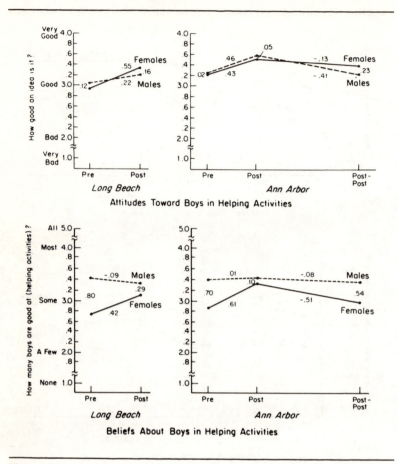

Figure 5.9 Persistence of Attitudes and Beliefs About Boys in Helping Activities

Beliefs about how many boys are good at these helping activities were very high initially for males (3.36, corresponding to an estimate between "some" and "most" boys). This estimate stayed fairly constant across all three points in time. Female subjects, in contrast, estimated at the pretest that many fewer boys were capable in this domain, but females were strongly impressed by *Freestyle*. Their posttest estimates were quite close to those of the boys. However, in the period following *Freestyle* they reconsidered their estimates, with a decay of 84 percent of the original effect. Thus, for female subjects at least, the decay in beliefs is again substantially greater than the decay in attitudes.

Girls and Boys in Leadership Roles. As Figure 5.10 shows, before *Freestyle* females were quite supportive of girls in leadership positions. Nonetheless, the series was able to augment this already supportive attitude by .25SD and this new level of support (3.41) persisted for the ensuing nine months. Males, on the other hand, started out quite negative toward girl leaders (2.20, or a "bad" idea. *Freestyle* shifted their attitudes .60SD, but it was to a level much lower than females' attitudes, and the attitude decayed 35 percent.

Figure 5.10 also shows the comparable data for attitudes toward boys as leaders. *Freestyle* was not trying to change these attitudes, but the data make an interesting point about the dynamics of change. Male respondents started out very supportive of boys as leaders (3.44) and their attitude remained stable across the 13 months. Both sexes, then, reached the same level of high positive support for leaders of their own sex. Freestyle led females to increase their support for boys as leaders (.60SD); in fact they became almost as supportive of boy-leaders as they were leaders of their own sex, and this attitude decayed only 18 percent. Males, as we saw, were not so persuaded. Males have more to lose, it might be argued. They currently dominate in adult leadership roles, and would have to relinquish actual positions plus sacrifice some group identity as well. In *Freestyle,* the "out-group" — boys — is the harder target to change in situations that involve a trade off of power.

Two conclusions seem warranted from the leadership data. First, *Freestyle* increased the general level of support for leaders of either sex, although the males still had a long way to go to be convinced that girl leaders are a good idea. Second, these effects persisted to a remarkable degree. The decay for attitudes ranges from 18 percent to 35 percent.

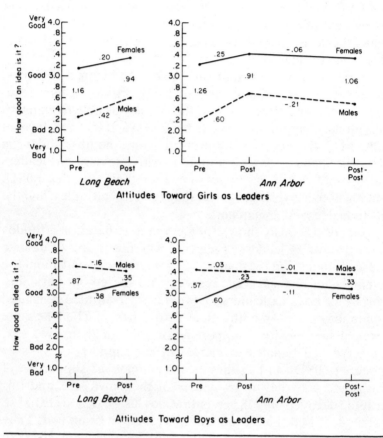

Figure 5.10   Persistence of Attitudes Toward Boys and Girls in Leadership Roles

When it comes to beliefs about how many boys and girls are good at leadership tasks, each sex defends its own group. Figure 5.11 displays the data. Females think "most" girls are good at being leaders and this belief is constant across all three points in time; males think the same about boy leaders. Before *Freestyle,* each sex thought that only "some" of the other sex were good leaders, and *Freestyle* increased this estimate by

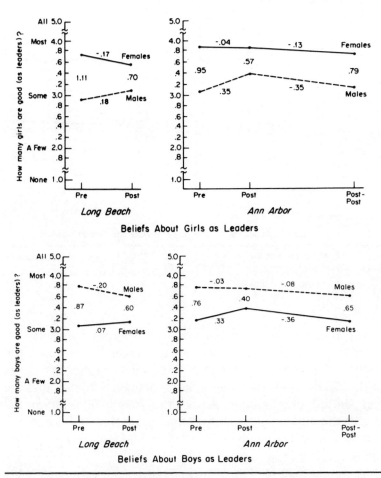

Figure 5.11   Persistence of Beliefs About Boys and Girls in Leadership Roles

about one-third SD. But in the ensuing nine months all of this effect disappeared. Unlike the corresponding attitudes, *Freestyle* had no lasting impact on beliefs about the leadership skill of girls.

Adult Job Roles. Freestyle's designers wanted to change the stereotype that some jobs are only for women and others for

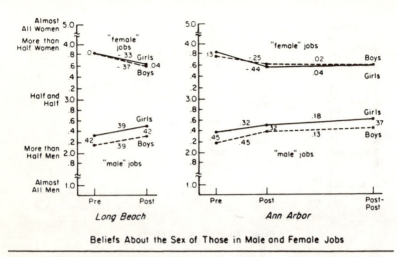

Figure 5.12 Persistence of Beliefs About the Sex of Those in Male and Female Jobs
NOTE: Scale on vertical axis is really two scales. As a result large effects (e.g., 44 SD) appear in the figure to be unusually "flat."

men. It was noted earlier that *Freestyle* was partially successful in this regard. The children were asked to estimate the
number of men and women in each of a list of jobs. Estimates
for the "male" jobs (mechanic, hotel manager, doctor, and the
like) shifted dramatically across the *Freestyle* intervention
period; the movement was from the "more than half are men"
point on the scale toward the "half men, half women" point (see
Figure 5.12).

A similar picture of movement occurred for estimates of the
composition of "female" jobs (nurse, secretary, and the like).
Figure 5.12 shows that this latter effect persisted perfectly
across the nine-month period subsequent to *Freestyle*. The
lack of decay for these beliefs leads to the speculation that
decay is much less likely if there is minimal exposure to the
relevant concepts during the post-intervention period. Children would undoubtedly have had more opportunities to

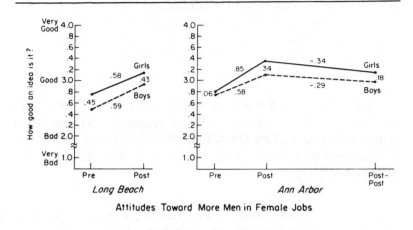

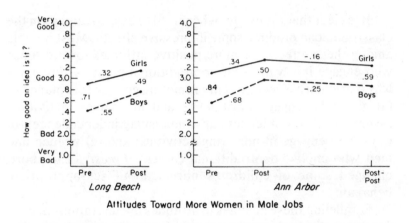

Figure 5.13   Persistence of Attitudes Toward Decreased Sex-Typing of Adult Jobs

observe and think about girls in athletics and mechanical activities than they would men in the jobs of nurse or secretary.

Attitudes toward increasing the proportion of men in "female" jobs and women in "male" jobs showed quite a bit of decay. Figure 5.13 displays the data. *Freestyle* had an unusually large effect on attitudes toward more men entering "female" jobs — .85SD for female respondents and .58SD for males. But the decay was 40 and 50 percent respectively. In one sense this decay is quite large; but the net effect across all three points in time is still quite high for girls (.51SD) and modest for boys (.29SD). Boys' attitudes after decay are still at the "good idea" level.

Attitudes toward more women entering "male" jobs were also influenced by *Freestyle*. Girls increased .34SD, an effect which then decayed by about half. Boys increased .68SD; the 37 percent decay for boys still left them with a very large net effect of .43SD.

CONCLUSION: THE EFFECTS OF INTENSIVE CLASSROOM USE

It is clear that *Freestyle*, when used to best advantage in the classroom, can produce some impressive effects. Most notable among these effects are more positive attitudes toward those who engage in a variety of nontraditional pursuits. *Freestyle* was particularly successful in promoting greater acceptance of (a) girls who engage in athletics and mechanical activities, assume positions of leadership, and display independence; (b) boys who engage in nurturing activities; and (c) women and men who choose nontraditional careers. *Freestyle*, in short, changed some of children's norms about sex-appropriate behavior.

Paralleling these changes in attitudes are alterations in children's beliefs about sex-role reality. *Freestyle*, for example, led children to believe that more girls are competent in mechanical activities and leadership roles than they originally thought, and that more boys are good at nurturing activities. *Freestyle* was least effective increasing children's interest in nontraditional pursuits, although we found subgroups of children whose interests changed by large amounts. Exposure to the nonstereotyped world of *Freestyle* is thus able to affect both children's attitudes about what is true of their world and their beliefs about what is true of their world; but it has more limited impact on children's interests.

The pattern of *Freestyle's* impact across the types of measured effects — attitudes, beliefs, and interests — is graphically summarized in Table 5.11. This table also summarizes *Freestyle's* impact across the three content themes and here too there is a pattern. Of the three content themes, behavioral skills proved to be most problematic. *Freestyle* altered children's beliefs concerning only one of the behavioral skills while it was successful in shaping many beliefs about both pre-occupational activities and adult roles. Similarly, the series did not produce as large changes in attitudes toward behavioral skills as it did attitudes toward childhood activities and adult roles.

Another content area which proved to be problematic was belief about who works to earn money to support the family and the corresponding attitude about who *should* do this task. Whether because *Freestyle* was not convincing or because such beliefs and attitudes are solidly anchored in personal experience, children simply refused to give up their conviction that husbands are, and should be, the primary breadwinners.

Freestyle's effects are certainly not unlimited. Yet for a 13-week classroom intervention, these effects are impressive in both scope and magnitude. Perhaps most impressive of all is the persistence of those effects which the series did achieve. Nine months after the conclusion of the intervention we returned to measure again the effects of *Freestyle* in one site. Two conclusions emerge from these longer-term follow-up data. First, there are some areas for which there is no decay at all, and a few others for which there is almost total decay. But the typical decay observed was in the range of 25-40 percent of the original effect. In most cases this decay is small enough to leave a residual net effect that is educationally significant. It appears from the *Freestyle* experience that prosocial television for children on a timely topic, when reinforced by classroom activities, is capable of inducing large changes in the attitudes and beliefs of children and that the method "inoculates" them fairly well

TABLE 5.11 Summary of Freestyle Effects on 9- to 12-Year-Olds Under Conditions of Intensive School Use

	Females	BELIEFS ABOUT	Males	Females	ATTITUDE TOWARD	Males	Females	INTEREST IN	Males
Childhood Pre-occup-ational Activities	•••	Boys in helping roles	no	•••	Boys in helping roles	•	inap	Helping	•
	no	Girls in athletics	••	•••	Girls in athletics	•••	•••	Athletics	inap
	•	Girls doing mechanics	•••	•••	Girls doing mechanics	•••	•	Mechanics	inap
		—			—		no	Science	inap
Childhood Behavioral Skills	a	Girls as leaders	a	no	Girls as leaders	•••		—	
	no	Girls being independent	no	••	Girls being independent	•••		—	
	no	Girls being assertive	no	a	Girls being assertive	a		—	
	no	Girls taking risks	no	no	Girls taking risks	no		—	
Adult Work and Family Roles	••	Sex of those in traditionally male jobs	••	••	More women in "male" jobs	•••	no	"Male" jobs	inap
	••	Sex of those in traditionally female jobs	••	•••	More men in "female" jobs	•••	••	"Realistic"	inap
	•	Wives doing male housework	•	•••	Wives doing more "male" housework	•	•	"Enterprising"	inap
	••	Husbands doing female housework	•	••	Husbands doing more "female" housework	•••	inap	"Female" jobs	no
	no	Wives support family	no	no	Wives support family	no	inap	"Social" jobs	•
	no	Husbands support family	no	no	Husbands support family	no		—	

KEY: — = the concept was not measured   inap = inappropriate for this audience
Size of Effect: ••• = large   •• = medium   • = small   no = not "educationally significant"   a = "homogenizing" effect only.

for at least nine months against a return to pre-intervention orientations. The examples of total decay point to the importance of careful selection of the topic and its treatment in the intervention package. The examples of partial decay argue strongly for incorporating "booster shots" into program designs.

Second, in the domains of childhood activities and behavioral skills, attitudes decayed much less than did beliefs. This was true in spite of the fact that larger initial changes were found for attitudes. As the world of *Freestyle* recedes into memory and children's own world reasserts its claim on them, beliefs about what is true return to their former levels more quickly and/or completely than attitudes about what is right. The world of *Freestyle,* it seems, has a less firm grip in what is true than on what is right.

NOTES

1. From Holland (1966: 16-17). Reprinted with permission of the author.
2. See DeFleur and Ball-Rokeach (1982) for an overview of relevant research.

Chapter 6

CHANGING THE AUDIENCE WITH MERE VIEWING

Freestyle yielded impressive effects when used with a classroom audience that discussed the meaning and implications of each show. But what happens if children simply view the shows and do not discuss them? We tested this kind of use in two ways. First we used a captive audience in a school setting. They were exposed to each show, but they did not discuss the shows afterward. Instead, they were released for recess or some other activity. This type of use is "unnatural," but it can tell us what is possible from mere exposure to all the shows. In a second, and more natural test, children viewed *Freestyle* at home during the weekly prime-time airing. While the setting was more natural, the probability of children missing shows was much higher. The only contrived aspect to this test was a weekly reminder from the classroom teacher to view the show at home. For both conditions students answered the same questionnaires discussed in the last chapter. This enables a comparison of effects of mere viewing with viewing supplemented with discussion.

VIEWING IN THE CLASSROOM

In the previous chapter we asked whether viewing-plus-discussion produced an educationally significant effect. In comparing view-only with viewing-plus-discussion we ask two questions: Is the effect of view-only educationally significant? What percentage of the viewing-plus-discussion effect is obtained with mere viewing? For answers to these questions we turn to data from Worcester and North Kansas City. In these locations schools were randomly assigned to the conditions of viewing-plus-discussion or view-only, thus permitting comparisons within locations of the effect of these two different treatments. In Worcester, schools were also assigned to a control condition; in North Kansas City there were too few schools to permit a control condition. As explained in Chapter 4 data are included in the following analyses only for students in classrooms where there was heavy viewing (24 out of 26 quarter-hour shows.) Demographics of the sample in these two cities can be found in Appendix C.

Before examining the overall picture, consider the example shown in Table 6.1. This shows beliefs of males about the competence of girls in mechanical activities. The first row shows the data from Long Beach that we discussed in the last chapter. Males started out believing that only "a few" girls were competent (2.07). After *Freestyle*, there was an increase that was statistically and educationally significant (.44SD). The second and third lines show the comparable data from Worcester and North Kansas City. The results for viewing-plus-discussion were the same or larger; the results for view-only were smaller. In both sites mere viewing resulted in educationally significant effects of .34SD. As a fraction of the view-plus-discussion effect this was 54 percent in Worcester and 83 percent in North Kansas City. To obtain a more stable estimate of effects we can average results from the two sites. This gives us an estimate of .34SD for view-only and .50SD for viewing-plus-discussion. (There were more boys in the Worcester sample, giving their estimate more weight.)

In the previous chapter our anlysis strategy was to determine if the experimental group differed significantly from the control group on the post test. If it did, then pre/post shifts of just the experimental group were examined to see if they were large enough to be judged educationally significant. In this chapter we need to take control group movement into account directly since we are interested in estimating the effect of

TABLE 6.1 Beliefs of Males About Girls in Mechanics: An Example Comparing View-Only and View-Plus-Discussion

	View Only			View + Discussion			View Only as Percentage of View and Discussion
Site	Mean Pretest	Mean Posttest	SD Difference	Mean Pretest	Mean Posttest	SD Difference	
1. Long Beach	NA	NA	NA	2.07	2.44	.44	
2. Worcester	1.96	2.20	.34	2.00	2.32	.41	54%
3. N. Kansas City	1.97	2.26	.34	1.97	2.46	.63	83%

view-only as a proportion of viewing-plus-discussion. The basic strategy involved adjusting the effect-size estimates for viewing-plus-discussion and view-only by any movement exhibited by the control group. This, in effect, would remove that portion of change which was not directly attributable to *Freestyle*. However, there was one complication in implementing this strategy. North Kansas City had no control group, and the Worcester control group exhibited wider fluctuations than controls in any other city. Accordingly, we averaged control group pre/post shift across four cities. We then subtracted the average shifts from the pre/post shifts of each of the two treatment groups. In most cases this resulted in little change for the estimate of effect size. But in some cases it increased the estimate (in the case where the control group declined from pretest to posttest), and in others it decreased it. After making this adjustment we averaged the effect-size estimates from Worcester and North Kansas City to provide more stable estimates of view-only and viewing-plus-discussion. In the example in Table 6.1, the average shift for males in the control group was a positive .12 scale units. This reduced the estimate of treatment effects from .34SD to .19SD for view-only and from .50SD to .35SD for viewing-plus-discussion.

Overall Effects

Consider first children's beliefs — an area in which viewing-plus-discussion showed a number of significant effects. The data are shown in rows 1-8 of Table 6.2. Beliefs about the proportion of girls competent in mechanical activities (row 1) showed a .36SD increase for females and .35SD for males in classrooms that discussed the shows. View-only yielded about half this effect for males, an effect that falls just short of the educational significance criterion of .20SD adopted for this study. For females, the view-only effect is three-quarters of viewing-plus-discussion and this is large enough to be categorized as a "modest" effect. For this one outcome area two things can be noted. Mere viewing yields effects that are smaller than desirable given *Freestyle's* overall goals, but impressively large when one considers that much less time and cost was required to achieve the effect. A similar conclusion applies for beliefs about girls in athletic activities.

The data on boys in helping activities (Table 6.2, row 3) illustrates a different point. Females who merely viewed the series did not change at all their estimates of boys' competence at child care and other nurturing activities. But those who had a chance to both view and discuss the series in class exhibited a large change. A similar point can be made about boys' beliefs about girls in leadership positions. The finding illustrates how difficult it is to make televsion dramas that by themselves are persuasive. There were many factors to consider in getting across an educational message including the complexity of the message, the explicitness of the message, and the relationship of the dramatic story line to the message. It is difficult to "get it all right" in every show. When an episode does not quite measure up, it appears that classroom discussion, at least in some circumstances, can compensate for its weaknesses.

Look now at the belief measures as a set. Using the criterion of .20SD for educational significance, we note that for females, viewing-plus-discussion (Table 6.2, column 2) yielded large effects for seven of the eight indices; on the eighth — girls in leadership roles — the beliefs of females were not really in need of change. Females who only viewed the shows reached the critierion of significant change on five of the seven indices. Typically, the amount of change was close to the threshold of educational significance and ranged between 45 and 90 percent of the viewing-plus-discussion effects. For boys, viewing-plus-discussion resulted in significant change on six of the eight indices while viewing alone worked for only three of the eight.

TABLE 6.2 Comparing View-Only with Viewing-Plus-Discussion

	FEMALES			MALES		
BELIEFS	View Only	View + Discussion	View Only as Percentage	View Only	View + Discussion	View Only as Percentage
1. Girls in mechanical activities	.26	.36	72	.19	.35	54
2. Girls in athletic activities	.21	.31	68	.21	.27	78
3. Boys in helping activities	.01	.36	03	-.07	.18	—
4. Girls in leadership roles	.00[c]	-.01[c]	0	.05	.24	21
5. Women in traditionally male jobs	.14	.25	56	.32	.14	229
6. Men in traditionally female jobs[a]	-.21	-.47	45	-.33	-.32	103
7. Wives doing traditionally male household tasks[a]	-.24	-.38	63	-.14	-.28	50
8. Husbands doing traditionally female household tasks[a]	-.36	-.40	90	-.18	-.43	42
ATTITUDES						
9. Girls in mechanical activities	.37	.49	76	.28	.48	58
10. Girls in athletic activities	.13[b]	.41	32	.10	.36	28

11. Boys in helping activities	.30	.61	49	.08	.40	20
12. Girls as leaders	.07c	.12c	—	.29	.40	73
13. More women in male jobs	.11	.37	30	.18	.35	51
14. More men in female jobs	.45	.69	65	.13	.45	29
15. Wives doing male household tasks[a]	-.00	-.22	00	-.08	-.17	—
16. Husbands doing female household tasks[a]	-.26	-.31	84	-.12	-.27	44
INTERESTS						
17. Mechanical activities	.27	.42	64	—	—	—
18. Scientific activities	.08c	.21c	38	—	—	—
19. Athletic activities	.17c	.28c	61	—	—	—
20. Helping activities	—	—	—	.06	.27	22

NOTE: Entries for "View Only" and "View + Discussion" are the weighted average of Worcester and No. Kansas City "SD Difference" figures for the experimental group adjusted by the average for control groups in all school-view cities. Entries for "View Only" are "View Only" divided by "View + Discussion × 100.

[a]Wording of question make negative values desirable.

[b]View Only girls were more approving than View + Discussion girls at pretest. Posttest scores were almost equal.

[c]Pretest scores were very high — not much room for change.

215

View-only effects ranged from 21-29 percent of viewing-plus-discussion.

Consider next the effects for attitudes (Table 6.2, rows 9-16). For girls, viewing-plus-discussion yielded large effects on all seven of the measures upon which there was room for change. For boys, it was seven out of the total of eight. Mere viewing resulted in effects larger than .20SD for only four of the seven measures for girls and two of eight for boys.

Finally, look at results for interests (Table 6.2, rows 17-20). Girls' interest in mechanical activities increased .27SD as a result of mere viewing and .42SD after viewing-plus-discussion. As we found in Long Beach and Milwaukee, all of this movement was at the "uninterested" end of the scale, but the movement was nonetheless large. In the scientific and athletic domains (Table 6.2, rows 18-19), there were modest effects for viewing-plus-discussion, although initial interest scores were high in these areas. Girls who merely viewed were below the threshold. Finally, for boys in helping activities there was a modest effect with discussion and almost none for mere viewing. The only adult job interests that were affected by mere viewing were girls' interests in the two mechanical jobs portrayed on the shows — car mechanic and machinist.

Under the ideal condition of exposing a captive audience to virtually all of the *Freestyle* shows, mere viewing appears insufficient to achieve the goals of the series. Nonetheless, it is noteworthy that none of the effects of mere viewing were negative. Boys, for example, were not antagonized by the series as might be evidenced by a growing negative attitude toward girls encroaching on the male domain. Further, a few measures showed an effect impressively close to that achieved with the help of discussion. Indeed, two areas showed as large or larger effects for view-only. This suggests that there is potential for dramas such as *Freestyle* to get across at least some messages without classroom mediation. Such potential perhaps can be further developed but it is likely that some issues will require girls and boys — and their teachers — to exchange ideas verbally before beliefs and attitudes will change.

VIEWING AT HOME

What happens when children are asked to view *Freestyle* at home on their local PBS station? Do they choose to view? Does viewing in this setting yield effects similar to those found for the viewers in our captive school setting? To answer these questions we studied two cities, Saginaw, MI and Covina, CA. In each district ten schools were selected to participate, with two participating classrooms in each school. Letters signed by each school's principal were sent home to the parents. The letter asked the parent to encourage the child to watch *Freestyle*. In some cases the parent was asked to encourage the child — but also to watch *Freestyle* with their child. Each week the classroom teacher reminded the class on Friday to watch the home broadcast. On Monday the students filled in a home-viewing chart which indicated whether they viewed and whether it was alone or with a parent. Using these data it was clear that parent co-viewing — supposedly a separate treatment — occurred equally frequently in both types of experimental conditions, leading to the conclusion that *experimentally* there was only one treatment: viewing.

Amount of Viewing

Show-by-show viewing behavior, based on the combined samples of Saginaw and Covina, are displayed in part 1 of Table 6.3. On the average, 32 percent of those asked to view watched any one show, with a high of 42 percent for the show "Flag" and a low of 21 percent for "Hey Mom!" It is hard to explain the variation. But the two shows with the lowest viewing were broadcast quite close to Christmas — a time when children are not in the classroom and seasonal activities and network specials provide competition for the activity of viewing *Freestyle*.

Overall, we interpret an average viewing rate of 32 percent as quite high — indicating that, with a good product, schools could achieve reasonable levels of home viewing with minimal effort. The data in Part 1 of Table 6.3 also indicate that the shows were more popular with girls than boys. *Freestyle's* messages are spread throughout an integrated 13-part series; what was the cumulative viewing behavior like? On the average, children watched only four out of the thirteen shows. Heavy viewers were more frequently girls.

Effects of Viewing at Home

To examine the effects of home viewing a slightly different strategy was required. We wanted to look at the effect size associated with different amounts of viewing. The research plan for home-viewing sites used the same random assignment procedure used in the school-viewing parts of the study. This yielded experimental and control groups that were comparable initially. But among those who were asked to view, self-selection operated to determine heavy and light viewers. This consideration, along with limited numbers of heavy-viewing children, led to our analyzing the data using a covariance strategy. Amount of viewing is the predictor. The dependent variables are the posttest scores on the various indices with the corresponding pretest scores "covaried" for each level of viewing. To test for an effect of viewing two criteria were used. One is the overall statistical significance of the analysis of covariance. The other is the statistical significance of one specific contrast: viewing of seven or more shows compared with any lesser amount of viewing. This is illustrated in Table 6.4, and the accompanying Figure 6.1, which show viewing related to beliefs about girls in mechanical activities. For girls in the study, the post-test mean scores are virtually the same for those in the control group and those who viewed less than seven shows. Girls who viewed seven or more shows shifted in the desired direction. The shift was statistically significant ($p < .01$)

TABLE 6.3   Viewing Behavior in Home Sites

| | Percentage Viewing | | |
| | Girls | Boys | Combined |
Episodes (in order of airing)	(262)	(248)	(510)
1. Partners	39	31	35
2. Cheers	37	31	34
3. Flag	47	37	42
4. Helping Hand	43	35	39
5. Scoop — Part 1	39	33	36
6. Scoop — Part 2	41	33	37
7. Hike	43	30	37
8. Variety Special (aired over Thanksgiving)	33	23	28
9. Candidates	38	24	31
10. Young and Old	32	20	26
11. Good Signs	30	19	25
12. Hey Mom	28	13	21
13. Grease Monkey	30	20	26
Average for 13 shows	37	27	32
Cumulative Viewing			
Zero shows viewed	24	32	28
1-3 shows	26	32	29
4-6 shows	18	19	18
7-9 shows	15	11	13
10-13 shows	17	6	12
Total	100	100	100

and educationally significant as well (.28SD). For boys, a shift occured only for the fifteen boys who were the heaviest viewers — 10-13 shows. We could conclude from these data that viewing at home achieved the desired effects for the heaviest viewers. This example shows the most powerful effects in the home-view data. Among the 20 outcome areas, significant effects were found for very few measures. The example above is the only one among the eight measures of beliefs. For the eight measures of attitudes, the only significant effect was a change in attitudes toward girls in mechanics, although there was a "tendency" in the data for boys who viewed 10-13 shows to

TABLE 6.4   Amount of Home Viewing Related to Beliefs About Girls in
            Mechanical Activities

	Females	Males
1. Overall test of equal means (F-test):	N.S.	N.S.
2. Contrast of viewing 7-13 shows vs. < 7 shows		
F-test	.01	N.S.
Raw difference	.21	.10
SD Difference	.28SD	.13SD

NOTE: Results are from analyses of covariance with six levels of viewing as shown in Figure 6.1.

become more accepting of adult women entering "male" jobs. For the four measures of personal interest in nontraditional activities there was only one significant shift. This was for girls' interest in mechanical activities; but it was only modest in size.

It is interesting to note that the changes all occurred for beliefs, attitudes, and interests regarding young girls in mechanical activities. They also were associated with women entering "male" jobs — a label associated with jobs such as car mechanic, truck driver, machinist, owner of a hardware store, and geologist. It appears that mechanical endeavors were the ones most convincingly portrayed on the shows, or perhaps the ones most amenable to change.

The Bottom Line for Mere Viewing

What do these findings say about the effectiveness of mere viewing? In the captive viewing study where children viewed virtually all the shows, there were a number of effects that were close in size to those achieved with viewing-plus-discussion. Of the remaining changes most were too small to value highly in terms of the overall goal of *Freestyle*, but all were in the desired direction. In other words, mere viewing does have some effects and these effects are all of the right kind. Production decisions could perhaps increase the size of these effects. These deci-

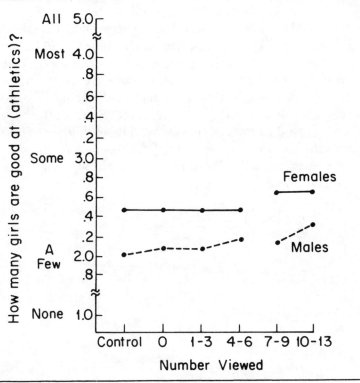

Figure 6.1 Amount of Home Viewing Related to Beliefs About Girls in Mechanical
          Activities

NOTE: Points are adjusted posttest means from analysis of covariance.

sions include careful choices of topics, adjustment of dramatic
story lines, and development of more shows devoted to a single
topic.

  In the home-viewing study several facts can be noted: effects were smaller; they were limited to outcomes related to
girls in mechanics; and they were limited to only the heaviest
viewers of the series. This may mean that the home viewing
environment is different in character; certainly viewing in that
setting is much less attentive. Whatever the dynamics, a view-

only intervention in the home would seem to require a heavier "dose" than the 13-show smorgasbord of *Freestyle*. How much more would be required cannot be answered with the data from this study. One strategy to increase the dose would be to produce more shows. Another possibility is to enhance the number who view existing shows at home. We were quite impressed that, with only minimal involvement of the school, very high levels of at-home viewing were achieved. Some of this viewing even involved parents coviewing with their children. This may represent an untapped potential for home broadcasts. We speculate more on this in the next chapter as we summarize the lessons of the *Freestyle* project.

Chapter 7

SOME IDEAS FOR FUTURE ARTISTIC EXPERIMENTS

The *Freestyle* strategy is to do what television does best. It does not explicitly instruct and certainly does not sermonize. Rather, it creates through drama an alternative world which embodies and makes real its messages. In the world of *Freestyle* children and adults competently engage in a variety of nontraditional pursuits. Their behavior comes to be accepted by others and is always richly rewarding. In this world, counterstereotypical behavior is commonplace, acceptable, and effective.

Though children did not understand everything they saw in the world of *Freestyle,* they did enthusiastically enter into it for short time each week. More importantly, they were changed by it. As a result of their brief residence in this world, 9- to 12-year-olds increased their estimates of the proportion of boys and girls who are competent in various nontraditional pursuits. Over time, children's own "real world" did seem to reassert itself; but even nine months after completion of the series, significant changes in children's beliefs about the competence of others remained. Exposure to *Freestyle* also helped children develop more positive attitudes toward others who choose nontraditional pursuits. These new norms for acceptable behavior were even more resistant than beliefs to decay over time.

Altogether, these results show the strategy of presenting an alternative sex-role reality is clearly effective in shaping children's own reality. The strategy is not without important limitations, however. One limitation is that the world of *Free-*

style was most influential when it could be interpreted and reinforced by teachers in the classroom. It was much less influential in classrooms where children could only view the series and could not discuss it with anyone. *Freestyle* was still less influential when children merely viewed it at home.

Another limitation of the strategy was its relative inability to affect children's own interests in nontraditional pursuits. It was not unreasonable to have expected *Freestyle's* images of childhood activities and adult occupations to have had some impact on children's expression of their own interests. As it turned out, however, these images affected only a few interests. It may be that televised activities and occupations, no matter how central to the story and how attractively portrayed, cannot powerfully affect most children's interests. These may be created and maintained by more concrete and powerful forces in children's lives.

A third limitation of the *Freestyle* strategy is that children's beliefs and attitudes within each of the three content themes covered by the series were not equally influenced. Beliefs and attitudes about behavioral skills, in particular, proved quite resistant to change. Here we must recognize two competing explanations for these relatively small effects. Perhaps, as with interests, certain beliefs and attitudes are firmly anchored in children's own life and experience and thus difficult to change. On the other hand, the messages about these complex behaviors were not consistently understood by children, so these may represent topics which are beyond the power of television to portray in one or two half-hour dramas.

In summary, the *Freestyle* strategy offers some promising successes as well as some fascinating failures. And because of both the successes and failures we think the strategy offers some useful lessons for further development of purposive, prosocial television. The first of these lessons, as we argued in Chapter 2, is that the development of such television is — and must be — a process less of engineering than of creation. The process is, and will continue to be, an experiment — but less a scientific than an artistic experiment.

The idea of artistic experiments draws attention to the work of the television professionals, but the idea does not deny the importance of contributions made by researchers and educators. Theories, research results, classroom experience, and the like cannot fully determine the work of the television professionals, but they can focus and direct their work toward important problems. This is also the contribution which the experiences of projects like *Freestyle* can make to the future projects. *Freestyle* does not provide formulas to solve the problems of the projects which follow, but it can help to identify worthwhile problems for which answers must be created. In our review of the lessons from *Freestyle* we will, therefore, identify some of the problems and issues which arise in the course of selecting project goals, designing a series, and planning for its effective use. There is no pretense of offering the right answers, only an attempt to identify the right problems.

SELECTING GOALS

Selecting goals which are both reasonable and worthwhile is among the first problems encountered by artistic experiments in prosocial television. This problem, in turn, has two aspects. One is the question of what goals are appropriate for television to tackle; the other is the process used to select among goals.

How to Select Goals

The experiences of *Freestyle* dramatically demonstrate that project goals and objectives do not emerge naturally from the general ideas that give rise to new projects. The setting of goals is not a process of deduction from general principles. The curriculum theorist, Joseph Schwab, argues that educators simply do not know enough about the learners, the learning process, and the material to be learned to devise theories from which curriculum can be deduced. Therefore, curriculum must be painstakingly pieced together into what he calls "an eclectic." The process for the development of this eclectic is neither inductive nor deductive, but rather deliberative:

> It cannot be inductive because the target of the method is not a generalization or explanation, but a decision about action in a concrete situation. It cannot be deductive because it deals with the concrete case not abstraction from cases and the concrete case cannot be settled by mere application of a principle.
>
> Deliberation is complex and arduous. It treats both ends and means and must treat them as mutually determining one another. It must make every effort to trace the branching pathways of consequences which may flow from each alternative and effect desiderata. It must then weigh alternatives and their costs and consequences against one another and choose, not the right alternative, for there is no such thing, but the best one [Schwab, 1969: 20].

"Deliberation" is perhaps too polite a term for what actually goes on in the process of setting goals. The experience of *Freestyle* suggests that disagreement on the interpretation of general ideas may well exist and that negotiation and compromise will be necessary. Planners and managers of the artistic experiment must come to terms with this political — or at least potentially political — nature of the process. Such a coming to terms requires planners and managers to consider who has access to the process and how they participate in it. In the case of *Freestyle* it could well be argued that too many groups and individuals had access to the process, at least during the original curriculum planning phase, and that such widespread participation was disruptive and counterproductive. Certainly the curriculum planning team itself was of this opinion. On the other hand, it could also be argued that the process ought to be accessible to those with a variety of ideas and expertise. Television professionals ought to contribute their judgments about the potential of their medium and researchers ought to contribute their knowledge of audience needs, predispositions, and the like. In addition, diverse intellectual, political, and moral points of view ought to be presented. Diversity is valuable even when efficiency is sacrificed. The issue of access to and participation in the goal-setting process is an issue of values as well as an issue of organizational design.

If planners and managers conclude that *optimum* access and participation in the process are not necessarily the same as *maximum* access and participation, then they must face the issue of structuring and controlling the process. Formal organizational structure is, of course, amenable to manipulation by project planners, but the *Freestyle* experience has shown that formal structure may be less influential than informal bases of power within the organization. Access to *Freestyle's* curriculum planning was widespread less because it was designed that way than because of the open nature of the curriculum planning task itself and the particular compostion of the curriculum planning team. There are important limits to what planners and managers can do. But even as *Freestyle* shows the difficulty of managing the process, it also suggests some ways for doing so.

A strategy for managing the politics of goal setting is suggested by *Freestyle's* curriculum revision phase. This phase of the project was more orderly than the original curriculum planning phase primarily because guidelines for revising the plan were developed and accepted. Paralleling the experiences of *Freestyle,* a project studied by the curriculum scholar Decker Walker (1971) made use of what Walker called a "platform" to set policy, resolve fundamental issues, and guide the work. For both projects, the guidelines or platform facilitated curriculum development by providing a foundation of shared principles and procedures. Vigorous deliberation was still possible but those who did the day-to-day work on the curriculum plan could proceed without extensive intervention by others.

If a platform is to be an element in the strategy to manage the goal-setting process, then planners and managers must actively promote its development. Walker reports that in the project he studied, the writings of the project leader established much of the platform and those who joined the project staff were likely to agree with its content. In *Freestyle,* on the other hand, only minimal work on anything resembling a platform was done before the project began. Further, some of the basic principles which had been established (for example, countering racial/ethnic stereotypes) were altered in the course of the project. Greater initial specification of principles and procedures on the part of the funder or other project initiators will help to structure and facilitate the work. Projects, in short, need constitutions.

Another element in a strategy to manage the goal-setting process is to explicitly consider and then purposefully acquire the necessary expertise for the task. In *Freestyle* the curriculum planning team lacked critical subject matter expertise — a fact which is surprising, perhaps, but understandable given the project's history and organization. This weakened the team's ability to specify the curriculum plan and made its activities more accessible to others. A strong curriculum planning staff, perhaps led by a strong leader as in Walker's project, would help tip the balance of power toward the curriculum planners. If planners could not completely specify the curriculum plan themselves, they would at least be able to serve as effective brokers of the demands made by others.

In summary, the *Freestyle* experience hardly provides a blueprint for the goal-setting process. The original curriculum planning phase of the project was particularly unruly. The curriculum revision phase was more speedy and efficient thanks to the development of guidelines, but that speed and efficiency was obtained, in part, through a mechanical and simplistic application of those guidelines. Yet even as *Freestyle* fails to provide the answer it clarifies the problem of goal setting as organizational politics.

What Goals to Select

The summative evaluation clearly shows that *Freestyle* did not accomplish all of its goals. The series had more of an impact on children's beliefs and attitudes than on their own interests in nontraditional pursuits. Perhaps this was because of the way in which pre-occupational activities and adult occupations were portrayed — shallowly and fleetingly. Perhaps it was because children's interests are difficult to reach with *any* sort of tele- vised message. Similarly, *Freestyle* did not have an impressive impact on children's beliefs and attitudes about most be- havioral skills. Perhaps this was because the abstract and com- plex nature of these concepts makes them difficult to convey via televison. The Ah-ha! scenes and the classroom discus- sions with teachers were apparently not enough to get the intended message to the kids. In any case, it is clear that expanding interests and promoting independence, assertive- ness, and risk-taking are difficult goals, and we cannot now be certain what should have been done differently.

These lessons from *Freestyle* are presented as inputs into the goal-setting processes of future prosocial television projects. They are not, however, presented as evidence that expanding interests and promoting complex ideas are unrea- sonable goals for such projects. On the contrary, they are presented as the most enticing problems to emerge from the *Freestyle* experience.

Goals that are worthwhile and difficult are just the sort of problems which can energize future artistic experiments. It is just such problems which can be the life force of a project, as *Freestyle* itself illustrates. Behavioral skills, from one point of view, represent a major failure of the project. From another point of view, however, they were central to the project's success. As the "figure" for most of the episodes, behavioral skills were central to the development of stories which commanded the attention of children and established the dramatic context for all the other messages about childhood activities and adult roles. Further, insofar as behavioral skills helped to make the series an active personal and social experience — as teachers told us it was for their students — these ideas contributed something of value in their own right. Behavioral skills were, then, a key creative problem which energized the *Freestyle* project and even today give dramatic life to the series. They are just the sort of problems which future artistic experiments should not avoid but rather seek out, come to understand more fully through deliberation and research, and then attempt to solve.

DESIGNING A SERIES

The design of a television series, like the choice of goals, offers challenges both as a process and as a product. Again, the problems of *how* to design and *what* to design both require creative solutions.

How to Design a Series

We have argued that *Freestyle* was created rather than engineered and that the executive producer more than anyone else was its creator. He translated the goals and objectives into messages and story ideas. He invented the figure/ground dramatic structure, the trial-and-reward plotline, and the other features of the series, and he oversaw scripting and production of each episode. *Freestyle* was fortunate in its choice of an executive producer whose abilities and experience enabled him to work effectively within the constraints imposed by the educational demands of the project as well as those imposed by the production machinery of television.

We hardly need to argue further for the centrality of creative television professionals to future artistic experiments. We probably do, however, need to emphasize that this does not deny a role to the educators and researchers. While it was the executive producer who solved many of the creative problems faced by the project, it was educators and researchers who formuluted or clarified many of these problems in the first place. The advisers could not determine the solutions created by the executive producer, but they did orient him to key problems.

In television production, project planners and managers must come to terms with this process of problem formulation and solution just as they must come to terms with the process of organizational politics in goal setting. Here again, planners and managers must consider who has access to the process and how they should participate in it. In television production, however, the problem is more likely to be facilitating access and participation rather than constraining it. The advisers must be given the opportunity to make their own unique contributions to the series design.

The attempt to solve this problem must come to terms with three specific issues. First, *Where* in the television production organization are the educators and researchers to gain access? In the *Freestyle* project, their access was limited to the executive producer who was the only television professional available to them. Direct access to writers, directors, and others could, however, be planned and budgeted into the project. This would bring a project a little closer to the ideal of true teamwork between the educators, researchers, and television professionals.

Second, *When* in the course of the production process are the educators and researchers to participate? In the *Freestyle* project, they participated in the design of the series only at those points in the process when the producer himself was required to make decisions. Direct access to writers and others, however, would generate opportunities for the educators and researchers to formulate and clarify the problems faced by these other television professionals.

Finally, *How* will they participate in the design of the series? In the *Freestyle* project some of the planned research was not used and some was not even conducted because of time and money constraints or simply because the executive producer could not use it. A plan for participation must, then, be based on a realistic appraisal of what is possible given the constraints of time and money and, more importantly, given the understanding that theory and research yield not the design itself, but rather the problems which must be solved by the design.

What to Design

The *Freestyle* series was designed not from ideas about how to change children so much as from a concern for the more immediate problems of designing a series which was acceptable to teachers as well as comprehensible and appealing to children. For example, the dramatic format emerged from the educators' concern for acceptance by classroom teachers. Arguing against the short segment format, the educators insisted that teachers of 9- to 12-year-olds did not want a fast-paced montage of cute lessons, but rather a compelling treatment of one or two ideas. The educators maintained that one sort of narrative format or another would be most appropriate for the messages of the project.

The summative evaluation affirms the educators' judgment in this. Classroom teachers did indeed find the *Freestyle* series to be useful and appropriate way to counter stereotypes. Many teachers praised the series for both holding the attention of their students and providing a worthwhile experience.

Teachers overwhelmingly said that they would recommend the series to others.

The largest stumbling block to teacher acceptance was that many teachers could not devote as much time to explicitly countering sex-role stereotypes as the series required. The infusion strategies for fitting *Freestyle* messages and materials into other curricular areas did little to alleviate the problem. The lack of time to devote to a particular educational goal is an aspect of educational acceptability which cannot be completely solved in the course of designing a television series and supporting materials. Perhaps, however, more effective infusion strategies can be developed. The problem of fitting curricular "add-ons" into the already crowded school day is, then, another of the tough but worthwhile problems which we commend to the hands of future artistic experimenters.

Appeal to children, especially boys, was another of the problems which influenced the work of the *Freestyle* developers and which was solved with some success. The dramatic format was promoted not only by the educators but also by the researchers who found 9- to 12-year-olds to be heavy viewers of programs with this format. Further, their testing of the three pilots showed the dramatic third pilot to be much preferred over the others.

The summative evaluation reaffirms these results. From the point of view of kids, *Freestyle* was good television. Children said that they enjoyed the series and compared it favorably to television viewed at home. The differences between boys and girls in this regard were small, although consistent home viewers tended more often to be girls. It is clear, however, that whatever the differences between boys and girls in appeal of the series, boys were not aggravated or repelled. Indeed, it was the boys who often exhibited the largest belief and attitude changes. While we cannot sort out the separate contributions of specific design features (characters, plotlines, and the like) to the series' appeal for children, we can at least say that *Freestyle* offers a model of purposive television which has solved the problem of appeal reasonably well.

This is apparently not the case with comprehension. This is a problem that the executive producer anticipated early in the design of the series with the idea that more screen time would have to be devoted to behavioral skills than the more easily visualized and symbolized pre-occupational activities. The researchers brought the problem into sharper focus with the idea that more explicit portrayal, rather than simply more screen time, was necessary for comprehension of *Freestyle's* complex messages. In response, the executive producer devised the Ah-ha! scene in which the behavioral skills and other concepts could be labeled and discussed. The print materials were also increasingly devoted to enhancing children's comprehension of the messages.

The summative evaluation suggests that these strategies were not consistently successful. Our analysis of three episodes of the series suggests in particular that some of the episodes were more comprehensible than others even though all were discussed in class. Further, the Ah-ha! scenes had only limited value because children tended not to incorporate them into their understanding of the story. Most interestingly, these results suggest that those episodes in which the messages were most intimately related to the story were the most comprehensible. The development of scripts in which message and story are one in the same is one of the most fascinating problems awaiting future artistic experiments.

Even if *Freestyle* was created less from ideas about how to achieve its ultimate goals than from a concern for more immediate problems, the series still offers a workable and quite successful strategy for achieving its goal of countering stereotypes. Central to this strategy is the use of television drama to create an alternative reality which can influence the beliefs and attitudes of its audience. In creating a new and different world, *Freestyle* has done what television does best.

And in *Freestyle,* what television does best has been put to good use. *Freestyle* harnessed the ability of television to make and remake the cultural worlds in which children — and all of us — live and has put that ability in the service of its particular educational goals. The primary creative problem for future artistic experiments is to embody their own particular goals in some new and different television world.

PACKAGING A COMPLEX TELEVISION INTERVENTION

Up to this point in our study of *Freestyle,* we have taken the fundamental ideas of the project pretty much for granted — for example, the fact that *Freestyle* was always intended to be a television series. The results of the summative evaluation, however, place us in a position to analyze and critique certain of these fundamental ideas. So in our final comments we will go back to the beginning — the most basic ideas of the project.

In 1975, the funder of *Freestyle* released the RFP soliciting proposals for the "TV Career Awareness Project" — a project which today we know as *Freestyle.* The RFP called for much more than a set of television shows. The funder in fact hoped to create the most powerful educational intervention to date. It recognized that stereotypes are shaped by a child's family, so a television series was needed that would reach families in the home. It knew that children would be more attentive in classrooms, so the series had to be acceptable to teachers. It suspected that television messages would be greatly enhanced with group instruction and stipulated that discussion guides be developed. It also called for the development of instructional activities which could extend the lessons beyond the short viewing and discussion periods. From the first, then, it envisioned a complex set of materials and activities which altogether could achieve the aim of "reducing the limiting effects of stereotypes." In these respects the project was more ambitious than anything before it. Perhaps Children's Television

Workship's *Electric Company* is similar in the number and complexity of materials developed, but *Electric Company* is devoted to improving reading, a cognitive activity with broad-based support of families and schools alike. *Freestyle* was unique in having such a diverse package of materials created for an educational effort in an "affective" area. With the evaluation data in hand, we can now assess the merits of this multifaceted approach — and raise a few more problems for future artistic experiments to tackle.

The One-Shot Approach

The *Freestyle* package is indeed rich and varied. But the implicit instructional model is still what we would call a "one-shot inoculation" against stereotypes. *Freestyle* is a single series of shows (along with supporting materials) of limited duration. It happens and then it is gone — forever.

Our persistence study suggests that belief and attitude change require more than this one-shot intervention, no matter how "potent" it is. If the goal is to maintain change, the more appropriate model is a two-or-three-part intervention similar to a vaccination model from medicine: an initial "inoculation" coupled with one or more "booster shots." One requirement of this model is sufficient materials to spread over two or more intervention periods. A more basic requirement is the breaking of the package, no matter how large, into complementary parts which can be used at different points in time; for example in two separate school years.

The notion is a familiar one in the elementary curriculum. In most subjects, such as social studies and math, the curriculum is a "spiral." That is, basic concepts are repeated as children progress through elementary school, but each time at a more sophisticated level. This model is less common for add-on interventions such as *Freestyle*. This notion is compelling because we now know that "spiraling" would be a more effective way to reduce stereotypes. On the other hand, it requires more time and greater effort at coordination than a single self-contained intervention. Thus, as this idea relieves one problem it exacerbates another.

Home versus School Distribution

The funder was attracted to the idea of delivering counterstereotypical messages directily into homes, but it was not sure that the message would be effective when viewed at home. It was more confident that school-based use would yield effects. Accordingly, it had both home and school versions created. The evaluation of *Freestyle* sheds some light on this dilemma faced by the funder in outlining the project.

Clearly, intensive school use was much more effective in changing children than any type of viewing alone. Indeed, we argue that an effective *pattern* of change requires the viewing-plus-discussion pattern of use. But we were impressed by two things in our studies of mere viewing. First, in our captive viewing study where children viewed virtually all the shows, there were a few effects that were close in size to those achieved with viewing-plus-discussion. Of the remaining changes, most were too small to value highly in terms of the overall goal of *Freestyle,* but all were in the desired direction. In other words, mere viewing does have some effects and these effects are all of the right kind. Some careful and creative work on the part of artistic experimenters could, perhaps, increase the size of these effects. The careful choice of goals which are most amenable to television treatment and/or most amenable to change will, no doubt, enhance effects. Beliefs and attitudes concerning girls in mechanical activities are examples of such goals from *Freestyle.* Also, the creation of television dramas which unite message and story as suggested in Chapter 3 will probably also enhance effects. But this is only part of the problem; getting the show viewed is the other and this leads us to a second observation from the study of viewing in homes.

With only a weekly reminder from their classroom teacher, fully one-third of the children watched *Freestyle* in their homes. This level of viewing is very high by PBS or even commercial network standards. PBS's children's shows typically draw well below 5 percent of the viewers. Our success in the evaluation raises the question whether innovative home-school linkages can be developed to enhance the amount and impact of home viewing. Teacher-encouraged home viewing could be coupled with classroom discussion of the shows. Prime Time School Television creates guides for some of the excellent stimulus materials on commercial television and is having modest success getting teachers to incorporate home-viewed television into their instruction. While it represents a nontraditional style of instruction for most teachers, it may be worth trying in future artistic experiments. This is especially true with curricular add-ons which are difficult for teachers to fit into a curriculum already filled with the "basics." Central to making this work is high quality shows which are suitable for prime-time broadcast. It is an expensive proposition to create "Hollywood quality" products for instructional purposes. But with today's students, reared on a heavy diet of shows with high production qualities, instructional programs need to have these same qualities to hold their attention.

Providing for Continued Use

Artistic experiments are just that — experiments. But each must be created with the expectation that it will be a success. If it is, at least two things will be necessary to ensure the continued use it deserves: resources for promotion and an "agent." Good materials sell themselves only after they have been brought to the attention of the many gatekeepers who make decisions about their use and are made readily available. No matter how good the materials are, they will do little good unless adequate resources have been set aside for promotion.

But, more than money, a long life for future artistic experiments requires ownership of the materials by an "agent" which takes responsibility for stocking, distributing, and promoting the series long after the product has its premiere. Television series need the equivalent of a publisher constantly looking after its interests. Multi-media efforts such as *Freestyle* face unique problems in this regard. Organizations such as Children's Television Workshop, (CTW) and the Agency for Instructional Television do this effectively for their own products. However, there are other television series, *Freestyle* included, which have been created by production houses whose functions do not include this distribution function. It is a herculean task for a funder to conceptualize the creation of a complex set of materials, let alone provide for support in perpetuity. But artistic experiments are too costly to have their successes hidden in books like this.

CONCLUSION

In developing the notion of artistic experiments we are arguing for the future of prosocial television. *Freestyle* has shown the power of this form of television. It has also shown some of its limits, but *Freestyle's* failures can rarely be interpreted unequivocally as limits of the medium. Rather they can easily be seen as challenges for which new solutions are needed.

We think there is a future for prosocial television, both because television can be a more useful educator than it has up until now and because there are more worthwhile goals to be accomplished. Indeed, expanding interests and promoting complex prosocial ideas are general goals which demand and are even now receiving attention from artistic experimenters. CTW's *3-2-1 Contact* is trying to enhance the scientific interests of girls and minorities. *Up and Coming,* developed with Emergency School Aid Act monies, is trying to enhance the skills of black teens to cope with the stressful challenges of growing up. But the possibilities for future artistic experiments are clouded by declining federal participation in education in general and in the production of purposive television in particular. Opportunities may arise from cable, disk, and other distribution systems, but that is far from clear. The profit motive may not coincide with the goals of this type of artistic experiment. Opportunities to conduct further artistic experiments may well be the most difficult problem for which creative solutions must be found.

Appendix A

FREESTYLE TELEVISION SHOWS
Synopses and Themes

SHOW 1: PARTNERS

Synopsis:

Penny and Marcus form a partnership providing household repairs. They learn from a quarrel over "who's boss" that cooperation (i.e., dividing the work and combining their various skills) is the best way to get the job done.

Themes:

(1) *Behavioral skill:* cooperation.
   Message: Cooperation is necessary to nearly all jobs and activities; it is more than merely "working together." It requires both a combination of skills and a division of labor. These are not always easily achieved and disputes may occur. These disputes, however, can be worked out.
(2) *Pre-occupational activities:* mechanical/technical activities for girls (specifically, home repair work including carpentry, plumbing, and electrical repair).
   Message: Girls can be competent in mechanical/technical activities.
(3) *Adult work/family role:* female hardware store owner/operator.
   Message: Women can be competent managers.

SHOW 2: CHEERS!

Synopsis:

Penny is on her way to becoming a cheerleader and Ramon is a member of the soccer team, but they also have a common interest: science. When they discover they must choose between their "traditional" activities and entering the science fair, their friends pressure them to choose the traditional activities. Penny and Ramon resist the peer pressure and go on to do a winning science project.

Themes:

(1) *Behavioral skill:* independence (specifically, independence from peer pressure).
   Message: Children often do what their friends want them to do. There is, however, satisfaction and perhaps also other rewards for doing what one is interested in doing even if one's friends do not approve.

(2) *Pre-occupational interests:* science for girls and minorities.
   Message: Science projects can be interesting activities and girls and minority children can succeed in them.

(3) *Adult work/family roles:* None are featured in this show although a science teacher is a supporting role.

SHOW 3: FLAG

Synopsis:

Denice proves her ability at flag football, but finds that the coach's wife and some members of the community don't like the idea of a girl on the team. Denice gets the support of her parents and friends and keeps on trying. In the big game she gets her chance and scores the winning touchdown.

Themes:

(1) *Behavioral skill:* None is featured in this show.

(2) *Pre-occupational activities:* sports for girls (specifically, flag football).
    Message: Girls can succeed in sports and other sorts of "nontraditional" activities as well.
(3) *Adult work/family roles:* sports-related occupations (e.g., coach).
    Message: Sports-related occupations besides professional athlete do exist.

SHOW 4: HELPING HAND

Synopsis:

Walter thinks tutoring math will be a cinch until he discovers that his pupil, newcomer, Dolores Cabrillo, can't read the math problems which are written in English. Dolores, fearing disgrace, swears Walter to secrecy and he and his bilingual buddy, Ramon, help Dolores prepare for her math exams. With their helping hands Dolores, of course, passes.

Themes:

(1) *Behavioral skill:* nurturing skills for boys.
    Message: Tutoring, like other nurturant activities, requires "helping skills" including empathy and patience.
(2) *Pre-occupational activities:* nurturant activities for boys (specifically, tutoring younger children).
    Message: Nurturant activities such as tutoring can be rewarding activities and boys can be competent in them.
(3) *Adult work/family roles:* teacher and other occupations related to tutoring.
    Message: If a child enjoys nurturant activities such as tutoring, there are a variety of occupations he or she may wish to consider.

SHOWS 5 AND 6 (two parts): SCOOP!

Synopsis:

"The changing roles of women and men in society" is the subject Denice and her classmates choose for their newspaper's feature story. Encouraged by their journalism teacher, the members of the newspaper club take sides in the attempt to show their town is either "fair" or "unfair." Denice as editor gets caught in the middle, but finally the newspaper staff finds that the roles of men and women are changing although there is still plenty of room for further change.

Themes:

(1) *Behavioral skill:* None is featured in this show.
(2) *Pre-occupational activities:* school newspaper work.
   Message: School newspapers offer a variety of interesting tasks including writing and photography.
(3) *Adult work/family roles:* Changes in family roles and a variety of occupational roles are featured.
   Message: Women are entering many occupations which have been sex-typed in the past and men are assuming more extensive family roles. There is still, however, much room for change in these areas. The program provides models of women and men in nontraditional occupations (e.g., male nurse, female doctor, female pharmacist, female bank officer) and nontraditional family roles (working mothers and fathers engaged in child care). The program also provides models of minority men and women in higher prestige occupations (small businessman and woman construction company owner).

SHOW 7: HIKE

Synopsis:

Walter persuades his younger sister, Tess, to take a reasonable risk in climbing some steep slopes to find rocks for her collection. Tess breaks away from the group and has to deal with being lost. Later, when Ramon takes an unreasonable risk and gets stuck on a dangerous ledge it's Tess who tells him to "be reasonable," climb no higher and help himself get rescued.

Themes:

(1) *Behavioral skill:* risk-taking.
   Message: Reasonable risks can be distinguished from unreasonable risks based on probability of success and degree of risk. Rea-

sonable risks are necessary if one is to learn about and enjoy new things. Unreasonable risks are pointless.

(2) *Pre-occupational activities:* science for girls (specifically, geology).
Message: Geology (i.e., rock collection and study) can be an interesting activity.

(3) *Adult work/family roles:* female geologist.
Message: Women can be competent in scientific occupations such as geology.

SHOW 8: FREESTYLE VARIETY SPECIAL

Synopsis:

This show is composed of a large variety of animated, filmed and taped segments. These segments are tied together by a troupe of four young entertainers who perform song and dance numbers and by guest host Mike Farrel, star of *M*A*S*H*. Each of these segments and numbers picks up one of the themes of the curriculum in an entertaining way.

Themes:

(1) *Behavioral skills:* each of the behavioral skills is touched upon briefly.
Message: Girls and boys should develop nontraditional skills.

(2) *Pre-occupational activities:* Each of the categories of nontraditional activities is touched upon briefly.
Message: There are a variety of nontraditional activities for boys and girls which they may enjoy.

(3) *Adult work/family roles:* Women in nontraditional jobs and fathers more deeply involved in family life are featured throughout.
Message: Traditional sex-roles of men and women are changing.

SHOW 9: CANDIDATES

Synopsis:

The candidates for seventh grade class president are Denice and big-man-on-campus, Tyler Speer. Denice seeks the advice of her local councilperson, Ms. Wilson, and gets some tips on responsible leadership that can help her with her campaign, her adult career, and her life.

Themes:

(1) *Behavioral skill:* leadership for girls.
Message: Leadership requires a number of skills including the ability to generate one's own ideas, the ability to listen to the ideas of others, and the ability to organize the tasks which need to be done.

(2) *Pre-occupational activities:* childhood leadership roles for girls (specifically, class president).
Message: Girls can exercise leadership skills and become competent leaders.

(3) *Adult work/family roles:* politics and other leadership roles for women.
Message: Leadership skills are necessary in great variety of occupations including politics. Women can be competent in these occupations.

SHOW 10: YOUNG AND OLD

Synopsis:

Marcus and Walter volunteer at a center for senior citizens as a part of their social studies assignment. Marcus puts his organizational skills to work and figures he'll have the seniors' recreational program in shape in no time. Marcus and Walter are surprised to find, however, that the seniors have "no time" for Marcus's arbitrary and overtaxing schedule. Marcus and Walter ask the help of the center's occupational therapist and learn about the importance of fully understanding the needs of others when trying to help them.

Themes:

(1) *Behavioral skill:* nurturing skills for boys.
Message: Any attempt to help another must be based on an understanding of the needs of that person.

(2) *Pre-occupational activities:* volunteer work for boys (specifically, volunteering in senior citizens center).
Message: Nurturant activities such as volunteer work can be rewarding activities and boys can be competent in them.

(3) *Adult work/family roles:* occupational therapist.
Message: Program reviews some of the duties of occupational therapists and emphasizes the importance of helping skills to this occupation.

SHOW 11: GOOD SIGNS

Synopsis:

A new student who is deaf is "mainstreamed" into the seventh grade class. She is received with a lack of compassion by the students, but it is Penny who takes the initiative to read about deafness, follows through by cultivating the new student's friendship, and finally speaks out firmly to the rest of the class on behalf of her new friend.

Themes:

(1) *Behavioral skill:* assertiveness for girls.
Message: Assertiveness requires that one take the initiative, follow through, and stand up for what one wants or feels is right.

(2) *Pre-occupational acitivities:* None are featured in this show.

(3) *Adult work/family roles:* None are featured in this show although a special education teacher for the hearing impaired is a supporting role.

SHOW 12: HEY, MOM!

Synopsis:

Walter and Tess's Mom, Kathleen, sees the need for another paycheck in the Dinsmore household and finds a job. To pave the way for her return to work she undertakes the task of teaching the family how to take care of themselves and each other by sharing household chores. Mr. Dinsmore is less than enthusiastic, but he eventually

notices Kathleen's increased self-esteem from her job and he realizes
that his working wife makes for a happier home — in which more of
his participation is needed.

Themes:

(1) *Behavioral skill:* None is featured in this show.
(2) *Pre-occupational activities:* household chores for children.
   Message: When mothers work the whole family has to take more
   responsibility for running the home.
(3) *Adult work/family roles:* female apprentice machinist, fathers and
   children assuming increased household responsibilities.
   Message: Traditional sex roles are changing. Women are entering
   non-traditional occupations and men are participating more fully in
   family life.

SHOW 13: GREASE MONKEY

Synopsis:

Chris is very interested in automobiles. She applies for a summer
job at a nearby gas station and convinces the crusty old owner to hire
her on her merits. While tending the station alone she takes on a job
that's too big for her and disaster follows. She summons up her
courage to return to work and a mechanic teaches her the fundamentals of auto repair. The next time there's trouble she's prepared to
handle it.

Themes:

(1) *Behavioral skill:* risk-taking.
   Message: Jobs for which one is not prepared are unreasonable
   risks. The same jobs may, however, be reasonable risks once one
   has had some training for them.
(2) *Pre-occupational activities:* mechanical/technical activities for
   girls (specifically, auto mechanics).
   Message: Girls can learn to be competent in mechanical/technical
   activities such as auto mechanics.
(3) *Adult work/family roles:* auto mechanic.
   Message: Auto mechanics can be an interesting occupation.

Appendix B

GOALS AND OBJECTIVES IN THE *FREESTYLE*
CURRICULUM PLAN[1]

The goal of the Television Career Awareness Project (TV CAP) is to expand, through an interrelated set of broadcast and nonbroadcast experiences, the career awareness of girls and boys aged nine to twelve by increasing their understanding of and influencing their attitudes toward:

- The relationship of current interests and activities to educational progress and career development;
- career opportunities; and
- sex-role stereotyping, and ethnicity as it affects sex-role stereotyping,

Sub-Goal 1. Children will learn to identify their skills and attitudes and relate these to potential career choices without the restrictions of sex-role stereotyping and ethnicity as if affects sex-role stereotyping.

    1.1   Children will be able to identify their existing interests, skills, and activities.

    1.2   Girls will be able to identify an increased number of nontraditional interests, skills, and activities (e.g., mechanical activities, spatial relationships, athletics, mathematics, science, and household tasks that require physical strength and/or exertion).

1.3   Girls will recognize that there are many non-traditional tasks and activities which they have the ability to perform.

1.4   Girls will be able to identify significant others who can perform nontraditional tasks and activities.

1.5   Boys will be able to identify an increased number of non-traditional activities (e.g., artistic; writing and skill with words; social service; child care; and household tasks such as cooking and dusting).

1.6   Boys will recognize that there are many nontraditional tasks and activities which they have the ability to perform.

1.7   Boys will be able to identify significant others who can perform nontraditional tasks and activities.

1.8   Children will be able to relate interests, skills, and activities previously considered nontraditional to occupations they know about and to potential career choices.

1.9   Children will recognize that sex-role stereotyping and its interaction with ethnic stereotyping restricts potential career choice.

1.10   Children will recognize that the bilingual ability of many ethnic minorities can create career opportunities which are equally appropriate for both males and females, e.g., international salesperson, translator, teacher, and international telephone operator.

1.11   Children will affirm their acceptance of boys and girls performing nontraditional activities.

1.12   Boys will identify or describe nontraditional activities they see themselves capable of performing.

1.13   Girls will identify or describe nontraditional activities they see themselves capable of performing.

1.14   After participating in the project, children will be able to develop an expanded list of interests and activities. This expanded list will reflect a reduced percentage of traditionally sex-stereotyped choices.

1.15 Children from ethnic minorities will indicate an interest in a greater variety of occupations.

Sub-Goal 2. Children will develop an understanding of the changing roles of men and women as adult workers and family members.

2.1 Children will recognize that girls and boys should prepare for future employment and be able to identify reasons why they should prepare.

2.2 Children will recognize that men and women work out of economic necessity and for personal satisfaction.

2.3 Children will recognize that men and women combine work and family roles for personal fulfillment.

2.4 Children will recognize that men and women who work can obtain positive rewards for themselves and their families from their jobs.

2.5 Children will affirm that it is acceptable for adult males and females to combine work and family roles.

2.6 Children will recognize that changes in work roles for women and men will complement, rather than restrict, changes in work roles for ethnic groups in this country.

2.7 Children, especially those from ethnic minorities, will recognize that in expanding work roles for males and females individuals need not lose their ethnic identity.

2.8 Children will recognize that in families where both partners work it is necessary for household responisbilities and child care to be shared.

2.9 Children will indicate that it is fair for adult males to assume a share of household responsibilities and child care.

2.10 Children will recognize that it is rewarding for all family members when fathers share in family responsibilities, including caring for children.

2.11 Children will affirm that caring for children can provide personal satisfaction.

2.12 Children will recognize that all members of the family benefit when all share in the financial responsibility for the family.

2.13   Children will recognize that the majority of girls will be gainfully employed 25-30 years of their adult life.

2.14   Children will identify a variety of nontraditional occupations as occupations for females.

2.15   Children will describe some of the duties, skills, training, and education necessary for nontraditional occupations for females.

2.16   Children will identify school subjects and/or interests and activities they have or know about which are similar to the skills required for specific nontraditional occupations for females.

2.17   Boys will affirm that it is acceptable for girls to choose nontraditional occupations.

2.18   Girls will be able to identify significant others (e.g., parents, teachers, girl friends) who have given them positive reinforcement for potential nontraditional career choices.

2.19   Given a list of careers for females, an increased number of girls will select nontraditional occupations they would like to explore.

2.20   Given a list of careers for females, individual girls will select an increased number of nontraditional occupations that they would like to explore.

2.21   Given a list of careers for females, boys will select nontraditional occupations they believe girls would like to explore.

Sub-Goal 3. Children, especially boys, will be able to identify helping skills, emotional expressiveness, and empathy for others and recognize how these behaviors relate to work and family roles.

3.1   Children will be able to identify appropriate emotions in a given situation.

3.2   Boys will affirm that it is acceptable to express their emotions openly.

3.3   Children will recognize that within certain ethnic groups the restrictions of sex-role stereotyping inhibit the open expression of emotions.

3.4   Children will accurately describe the feelings of others in given situations.

3.5   Children will be able to compare and contrast the feelings of others with their own.

3.6   Children will affirm that it is good to respect the feelings of others.

3.7   Children will be able to identify ways in which they can help others.

3.8   Children will be able to identify instances when others need help.

3.9   Having identified situations in which others need help, children will recommend ways in which help can be provided.

3.10   Children will identify a variety of nontraditional occupations for males which require helping behavior.

3.11   Children will describe some of the duties, skills, training, and education necessary for nontraditional occupations for males.

3.12   Children will identify school subjects and/or interests and activities they have or know about which are similar to the skills required for nontraditional occupations for males.

3.13   Girls will affirm that it is acceptable for boys to choose nontraditional occupations.

3.14   Boys will be able to identify significant others (e.g., parents, teachers, boyfriends) who have given them positive reinforcement for potential nontraditional career choices.

3.15 Given a list of careers for males, an increased number of boys will select nontraditional occupations they would like to explore.

3.16 Given a list of careers for males, individual boys will select an increased number of nontraditional occupations they would like to explore.

3.17 Given a list of careers for males, girls will select nontraditional occupations they believe boys would like to explore.

Sub-Goal 4. Children will learn about selected behavior strategies, such as independence, initiative, self-direction, assertiveness, and cooperation and how these strategies influence educational progress and occupational preparation. Independence, initiative, and self-direction are especially important for girls.

4.1 Children will identify the ways in which independence can be used as an aid to achievement.

4.2 Children will affirm that independence can be an appropriate strategy to use in achieving a goal.

4.3 Children will identify the ways in which initiative can be used as an aid to achievement.

4.4 Children will affirm that initiative can be an appropriate strategy to use in achieving a goal.

4.5 Children will identify the ways in which self-direction can be used as an aid to achievement.

4.6 Children will affirm that self-direction can be an appropriate strategy to use in achieving a goal.

4.7 Children will identify the ways in which assertiveness can be used as an aid to achievement.

4.8 Children will affirm that assertiveness can be an appropriate strategy to use in achieving a goal.

4.9 Children will identify the ways in which cooperation can be used as an aid to achievement.

4.10 Children will affirm that cooperation can be an appropriate strategy to use in achieving a goal.

Sub-Goal 5. Children, especially girls will recognize that taking responsibility and providing responsible leadership are essential to educational progress and career development.

5.1 Children will be able to identify some elements of responsibility.

5.2 Children will be able to identify ways in which one can become a responsible person.

5.3 Children will recognize some of the behaviors involved in assuming responsibility.

5.4 Children will recognize that both boys and girls, regardless of ethnic background, are capable of exhibiting responsible behaviors.

5.5 Children will be able to identify instances in which they exhibited responsibility.

5.6 Children will affirm that it is necessary to exhibit responsible behaviors to reach a career goal.

5.7 Girls will be able to perceive themselves in responsible career roles.

5.8 Children will be able to identify some elements of responsible leadership.

5.9 Children will recognize that both boys and girls, regardless of ethnic background, are capable of providing responsible leadership.

5.10 Children will affirm that it is appropriate for girls to assume responsible leadership positions.

5.11 Children will be able to identify careers, or career roles, in which being a responsible leader is a vital factor.

Sub-Goal 6. Children will recognize that taking reasonable risks and learning how to cope with the success and/or failure that results from taking risks are necessary for educational progress and career development.

6.1 Children will be able to identify both reasonable and unreasonable risks.

6.2   Children, especially girls, will recognize that reasonable risks are a necessary part of achievement.

6.3   Children will affirm reasonable risk-taking when appropriate to accomplish a goal.

6.4   Children will recognize that it is difficult for boys and girls from certain ethnic or socioeconomic groups to take reasonable risks because they fear rejection.

6.5   Girls will recognize that success is due primarily to effort, ability, and self-esteem rather than luck.

6.6   Girls will be able to identify or describe personal situations in which their success was due to their ability and effort.

6.7   Girls will affirm that it is acceptable to take pleasure in recognition of their accomplishments by others.

6.8   Children will recognize that failure is caused.

6.9   Children will recognize that failure can be coped with by:

1. analyzing what they might have done differently;

2. recognizing that they should not have tried the task;

3. asking for help when they need it; and then

4. trying again.

6.10 Given a failure situation, after anlysis and if appropriate, children will try again using an alternative course of action.

NOTE

1. The following is excerpted from "Curriculum for the Television Career Awareness Project 'Freestyle' — a Television Series for Grades 4-5-6." Los Angeles: Office of the Los Angeles County Superintendent of Schools, 1978.

Appendix C

TABLE C.1 Demographics After Eliminating Low Implementing Classrooms

	Treatment n	%	Sex n	%	Grade n	%	Race n	%
Long Beach/Torrance (N = 948)								
Control	363	38	Girls 435	46	Four 310	33	White 649	69
View + Discussion	585	62	Boys 513	54	Five 237	25	Black 155	16
					Six 401	42	Mexican 144	15
Milwaukee (N = 1031)								
Control	247	24	Girls 535	52	Four 364	35	White 567	55
View + Discussion	784	76	Boys 496	48	Five 311	30	Black 317	31
					Six 356	35	Hispanic 147	14
Ann Arbor (N = 589)								
Control	477	19	Girls 283	48	Four 229	39	White 412	70
View + Discussion	112	81	Boys 306	52	Five 96	16	Black 148	25
					Six 264	45	Other 29	5
Worcester (N = 1064)								
Control	268	25	Girls 518	49	Four 368	35	White 1030	97
View only	375	35	Boys 546	51	Five 347	33	Black 33	3
View + Discussion	421	40			Six 349	33	Other 1	*

(continued)

TABLE C.1 continued

	Treatment			Sex			Grade			Race	
	n	%		n	%		n	%		n	%
North Kansas City (N = 555)											
View only	245	44	Girls	290	52	Four	152	27	White	548	99
View + Discussion	310	56	Boys	265	48	Five	176	32	Other	7	1
						Six	227	41			
Saginaw (N = 351)											
Control	99	28	Girls	182	52	Four	189	54	White	266	76
Home View	252	72	Boys	169	48	Five	41	12	Black	62	18
						Six	121	34	Mexican	19	5
									Other	4	1
Covina (N = 427)											
Control	112	26	Girls	211	49	Four	227	53	White	315	74
Home View	315	74	Boys	216	51	Six	200	47	Black	4	1
									Mexican	97	23
									Other	11	2

TABLE C.2 Cross-Time Shifts in Ann Arbor Experimental Persisters

OUTCOME	Total		Females				Males			
	T1 Mean (a)	T1 SD (b)	T1 Mean (c)	T2-T1 b (d)	T3-T2 b (e)	e/d as pct (f)*	T1 Mean (g)	T2-T1 b (h)	T3-T2 b (i)	i/h as pct (j)*
Childhood Activities										
1. Att twd girls in mech	2.78	.78	2.94	.46	.01	+02	2.64	.47	−.14	−30
2. Belief about girls in mech	2.26	.78	2.53	.30	−.18	−60	2.03	.59	−.24	−41
3. Att twd girls in ath	3.01	.87	3.43	.21	−.07	−33	2.65	.51	−.12	−24
4. Belief about girls in ath	2.86	.81	3.20	.19	−.07	−37	2.57	.59	−.25	−42
5. Att twd boys helping	3.25	.61	3.25	.43	−.13	−30	3.26	.46	−.41	−89
6. Belief about boys helping	3.10	.79	2.81	.61	−.51	−84	3.36	.01	−.08	a
Behavioral Skills										
7. Att twd girls as ldrs	2.67	.80	3.21	.25	−.06	−24	2.20	.60	−.21	−35
8. Belief about girls as ldrs	3.40	.84	3.83	−.04	−.13	a	3.03	.35	−.35	−100
9. Att twd boys as ldrs	3.16	.70	2.84	.60	−.11	−18	3.44	−.03	−.01	a
10. Belief about boys as ldrs	3.45	.83	3.14	.33	−.36	−109	3.71	−.03	−.08	a

(continued)

259

TABLE C.2 continued

OUTCOME	Total		Females				Males			
	T1 Mean (a)	T1 SD (b)	T1 Mean (c)	T2-T1 b (d)	T3-T2 b (e)	e/d as pct (f)*	T1 Mean (g)	T2-T1 b (h)	T3-T2 b (i)	i/h as pct (j)*
Adult Job Roles										
11. Belief about sex of those in male jobs	2.22	.38	2.31	.32	.18	+56	2.15	.45	.13	+22
12. Att twd more women in male jobs	2.62	.66	2.87	.34	-.16	-47	2.40	.68	-.25	-37
13. Belief about sex of those in fem jobs	3.78	.48	3.81	-.44	.04	-09[b]	3.75	-.25	.02	-08[b]
14. Att twd more men in fem jobs	2.78	.61	2.80	.85	-.34	-40	2.76	.58	-.29	-50

NOTE: Table includes only children in high implementing classrooms who provided data at all three points in time (n = 280).

a Initial effect too small to calculate decay as a percentage.

b Scale is reversed; negative shift indicates a positive effect.

*This column presents decay as a percentage of initial effect.

Bibliography

BERGER, P.L. and T. LUCKMAN (1966) The Social Construction of Reality. New York: Doubleday.

COHEN, J. (1977) Statistical Power Analysis and the Behavioral Sciences. New York: Academic.

CRONBACH, L. (1976) "Research on classrooms and schools: formulation of questions, design, and analysis." Occasional Papers of the Stanford Evaluation Consortium, Stanford University.

DeFLEUR, M.L. and S. BALL-ROKEACH, (1982) Theories of Mass Communication. New York: Longman.

DIRR, P.J. and R.J. PEDONE (1979) Uses of Television for Instruction, 1976-77. Final Report of the School TV Utilization Study. Washington, DC: National Center for Educational Statistics.

ETTEMA, J.S. (1980) Working Together: A study of Cooperation Among Producers, Educators, and Researchers to Create Educational Television. Ann Arbor: Institute for Social Research.

GERBNER, G. and L. GROSS (1976) "Living with television: the violence profile." Journal of Communication 26: 173-194.

GUTTENTAG, M. and H. BRAY (1976) Undoing Sex Stereotypes. New York: McGraw-Hill.

HIRSCH, P.M. (1980) "The scary world of the nonviewer and other anomolies: a reanalysis of Gerbner et al's findings on cultivation analysis, part I." Communication Research 7: 403-456.

HOLLAND, J. (1966) The Psychology of Vocational Choice. Waltham; MA: Blaisdell.

HORST, D.P. and G.K. TALLMADGE (1976) A Practical Guide to Measuring Project Impact on Student Achievement. Washington: U.S. Office of Education.

JOHNSTON, J. (1981) "Evaluation of curriculum innovations: a product validation approach." in C. Aslanian (ed.) Improving Educational Evaluation Methods. Beverly Hills: Sage.

———, J. ETTEMA, and T. DAVIDSON (1980) An Evaluation of Freestyle: A Television Series to Reduce Sex-Role Stereotypes. Ann Arbor: Institute for Social Research.

KOB, J. (1975) Begleituntersuchung zur Ferneshserie Sesamstrasse. Hamburg, Germany: Hans Bredow Institute.

LAND, H. W. (1971-1972) The Children's Television Workshop: How and Why It Works. Jericho, NY: Nassau Board of Cooperative Educational Services.

LEIFER, A. D. and G. S. LESSER (1976) The Development of Career Awareness in Young Children. Washington, DC: National Institute of Education.

LESSER, G. S. (1974) Children and Television: Lessons From Sesame Street. New York: Vintage.

National Institute of Education, (1975) TV Career Awareness Project Request for Proposal. Washington, DC: National Institute of Education.

PREDIGER, D. J., J. D. ROTH, and R. J. NOETH (1973) A Nationwide Study of Student Career Development: A Summary of Results. Iowa City: American College Testing Program.

SCHWAB, J. S. (1969) "The practical: a language for curriculum." School Review 78: 1-23.

TALLMADGE, G. K. (1977) Joint Dissemination Review Panel, Ideabook. Washington, DC: National Institute of Education.

TOMLINSON, T. and D. TenHOUTEN, (1973) "System awareness, exploitive potential and ascribed status of elites." Presented to the American Psychological Association Annual Meeting, Montreal.

TRIANDIS, H. C. (1971) Attitude and Attitude Change. New York: John Wiley,

WALKER, D. F. (1971) "A naturalistic model for curriculum development." School Review 80: 51-65.

WILLIAMS, F., R. LaROSE and F. FROST (1981) Children, Television and Sex-Role Stereotyping. New York: Praeger.

WISE, R., I. CHARNER, and M. L. RANDOUR (1976) "A conceptual framework for career awareness in career decision making." Counseling Psychologist 6: 47-53.

About the Authors

Jerome Johnston is Associate Research Scientist at the University of Michigan's Institute for Social Research. His research interests include instructional technology, program evaluation, and developmental psychology. He has co-authored two books on adolescence (*Adolescence to Adulthood* and *Young Men and Military Service*) and has book chapters in educational evaluation ("Evaluation of Curriculum Innovations: A Product Validation Approach") and communication ("Using Television to change Stereotypes").

James S. Ettema is Assistant Professor of Journalism at the University of Minnesota. His research interests focus on process and effects in communication. He is author of *Working Together: A study of Cooperation Among Producers, Educators, and Researchers to Create Educational Television* and co-editor of *Individuals in Mass Media Organizations: Creativity and Constraint.*